How to
Raise a
Successful
Daughter

How to Raise a Successful Daughter

Barbara Powell

Nelson-Hall 🔳 Chicago

Library of Congress Cataloging in Publication Data

Powell, Barbara, 1929-
How to raise a successful daughter.

Bibliography: p.
Includes index.
1. Daughters.   2. Children—Management.   I. Title.
HQ777.P68   649'.133   78-16975
ISBN 0-88229-457-1 (cloth)
ISBN 0-88229-679-5 (paper)

Manufactured in the United States of America

10   9   8   7   6   5   4   3   2   1

Contents

Introduction

1. What Is a Successful Daughter?   1

2. A Forecast of Your Daughter's Life   11

3. Avoiding Sexual Stereotypes   21

4. Building Self-Confidence   33

5. Developing Independence   43

6. Enhancing Achievement Efforts   55

7. Providing Role Models   63

8. History Lessons   71

9. Fathers and Daughters   87

10. Having a Small Family   93

11. Encouraging Early Interests   101

12. Equal Education?   111

13. Adolescent Conflicts about Success   121

14. College and Coeducation   129

Notes and References   135

Index   141

To my son, Rich

who has successfully survived a feminist household
and held his own with three successful sisters

Acknowledgments

I would like to express my indebtedness to my parents, who raised me to strive for success; to Ida Davidoff, who has been my role model, mentor, and friend for many years; to Wellesley College, which helped me to grow intellectually and develop strength for the future during my undergraduate years; to Marvin Reznikoff, for his encouragement and support throughout my doctoral program, which was so important to me in achieving my goals; to Elizabeth Granfield and Sharon Corsiglia, for their friendship and support in this endeavor as well as in many others; to my daughters, Susan, Jenny, and Julie, for their helpful comments and suggestions on this topic and this manuscript; to my son Rich for helping to balance things out with the masculine point of view, and to all of my children for the insights and satisfactions I have experienced and continue to experience as their mother. I want to thank Julie in particular for her careful assistance in typing and proofreading the manuscript.

Introduction

This book could perhaps have been titled *How to Raise a Successful Person*. Raising a daughter to be successful—and by that I mean a specific kind of personal success, not the "good wife and mother" that has been equated with being a successful woman in the past—requires more or less the same kind of parenting that produces successful sons.

However, most books about raising children—in fact, all of them that have come to my attention—are really about raising boys, with a few peripheral comments addressed to parents of female children. And besides, there are some kinds of things parents do which seem to produce different results in boys and girls. That is why I am writing this book specifically for you who have daughters and would like them to grow up to be successful.

Most of us who are old enough to be parents now grew up with certain expectations about girls, boys, men, and women, and most of us accepted these stereotyped concepts without challenge. The past decade has introduced many changing ideas about what women can do and be. But it is my personal feeling that at the level where most personality development actually occurs—during the preschool years—the past is still very much with us.

A recent rereading of the most popular guidebooks for parents on the market today, in 1978, has convinced me that much more is needed than changing the "he" to "she" (or "it") if we are to avoid passing on to our children the sexual stereotypes that are so handicapping to women. A girl brought up first to be a girl, and second (usually a poor second) to be a person, will never be free to develop her own abilities and make whatever contribution to society—other than the raising of children— she has the capacity to make. It has been the misfortune of American women for several decades to be educated for equality, yet subtly pushed toward the kind of passivity and dependency which our culture considers desirable for women. These characteristics are insurmountable obstacles to success in any demanding profession or high level creative endeavor.

It has been a number of years since my own four children, three of them girls, were small, and I am the first to admit that I have made all kinds of mistakes in bringing them up. When my oldest daughter was born, in 1955, it hadn't occurred to me to care whether Dr. Spock referred to babies as "he," "she," or "it." Now that she is twenty-two, and my younger daughters nineteen and eighteen, my own consciousness has risen and I have learned much about the early socialization of children in my studies and in my work as a clinical psychologist.

As a result, I feel increasingly certain that the inequalities between the sexes can be traced not so much to the culture or the school, though these factors are admittedly of great importance, as to early training and experience at home. Girls must learn from early childhood that they are valuable as *people* and that their sex will not in any way limit the possibilities open to them. Except in a few isolated cases, this is not what has been happening.

Of course boys have to be brought up to treat girls like people, not just girls—but that is not the topic of this book. In families where girls are being raised as people, boys will accept them as such, and the men they grow into will encourage and help their mates to be doctors and lawyers, architects and engineers, policewomen and politicians. I hope your daughter will be among them.

This, then, is a book about raising daughters first of all to be successful people, to follow their talents wherever they lead them, and to be free to explore the world of intellect and achievement which has in the past been truly open only to men and to a few very unusual women.

I
What Is a Successful Daughter?

Of course there is no one opinion as to what constitutes a successful daughter. There is even some confusion about what constitutes a successful person—but not as much. Some definitions of success may require only that a person be happy and well adjusted. Usually, though, a "success" means someone who is doing well in his job or profession, and enjoys a position and income appropriate to his age, education, and experience.

Note that I said "his."

I did so deliberately to emphasize the fact that we are not accustomed to defining success for women in the same terms, even though ours is a success-oriented society. In fact, we are apt to define a woman in terms of her husband's success, not her own. Many women, probably the majority, still think of themselves in this way. And no wonder. This is the way we (most of us, anyway) were conditioned to think from earliest childhood.

1

Most of our parents probably felt that we would be successful as daughters and as women if we turned out to be good wives and mothers. (There have always been some parents who felt otherwise, and I will have a lot to say about them later.) I think there is a dangerous fallacy in this thinking, for it means that half the race—the female half—will always be secondary to the other half, raising up generation after generation of children of which only the males will be expected to produce anything except more children.

It doesn't seem reasonable to educate women like men and then expect them to be contented in the traditional role of women at home. I have personally experienced the frustrations which occur when a woman who has been educated to think like a man has to start acting like a woman. Though there were some rewards, I do not look back with pleasure on the years when I was a full-time housewife. And I hope that my daughters will never live as I lived during those years. In my work as a vocational counselor and psychologist, I have talked with many other women who feel similarly frustrated and who hope their daughters will lead different kinds of lives.

Not all women share these feelings, of course. Many are happy, or say they are, in the traditional role our society assigns to women. I do not see many of them because women who come for counseling are those who are not satisfied with their lives. Perhaps there will always be women who prefer to stay at home and occupy themselves with their domestic responsibilities. But I think that with each generation there will be fewer and fewer of them.

The fact is, there are fewer and fewer already. More than half of all women aged eighteen to sixty-four are working outside the home right now. So it just doesn't seem sensible to raise your daughter to think that her role in life is to be a wife and mother. She may be that, but she will probably be something else too, and for longer. The problem is that women seldom realize what lies ahead of them, and don't prepare for it. Do we really want to bring up another generation of women who have to have their consciousness raised? I don't think so.

I frequently hear (and read) the insistence, often even on the part of feminists, that the meaning of liberation is that women should be free to stay home and be traditional wives and mothers if that is what they prefer. Personally, I do not agree that this will continue to be a viable option for middle-and upper middle-class women. For my own generation, it has been and still is, but I do not see it in the years ahead for my daughters or for yours. How can a healthy, intelligent, and well-educated woman choose to devote herself entirely to a home containing at the most two children who will be in school all day by the time she is thirty-five or forty?

In my terms, then, raising a successful daughter means raising one who will make the most of her potential, whatever it may be. She is someone who will find a meaningful role for herself *outside the home*. She may or may not marry, for this is a choice women are increasingly free to make, and increasing numbers of women are now choosing to remain single. (In the twenty to twenty-four age bracket, there has been an increase from 28 percent in 1960 to 54 percent in 1977 in the number of women who have remained single.)[1] She will choose a career or profession which will allow her to use her abilities, whatever they may be, to the fullest. I don't think she will choose volunteer work, the traditional outlet of upper middle-class women, because this seldom gives lasting satisfaction or feelings of self-worth and is not readily translatable into a paid career. From a financial point of view it is only sensible for the *independently* wealthy woman. As I see it, then, your daughter's success will be measurable in terms of what she herself has accomplished, not what her husband or children have done. Do you want any less than this for her?

Even using this relatively broad definition, it is not easy today to find many women who are successful. Most women simply haven't even thought of themselves as candidates for success. We haven't tried to enter challenging careers because no matter how bright we are, most of us have up to now assumed we would just get married so it really didn't matter what we did anyway. A lot of this is due to the attitudes and expectations we learned from our mothers and fathers.

When more demanding definitions of success are applied, it becomes even more difficult to find women who meet the criteria. Recently a group of women scientists decided to have a conference on women and success in scientific fields and other professions, such as architecture, where men have predominated. They established as a working definition of success "the ability to function in a chosen profession with some measure of peer recognition." Finding women in top-level positions, especially in the sciences, proved to be quite difficult. Most women in top-status positions are in fact at the *bottom* of the top. An additional and unexpected problem in planning the conference was that a few of the women invited to participate declined because they didn't want to be publicly labeled "successful." It appeared that they were actually embarrassed by this designation.[2]

Matina Horner, the president of Radcliffe College, believes that women fear success and that this fear accounts for the fact that few women have managed to achieve at high levels. She measured fear of success by asking subjects to write stories based on the cue, "After first term finals, Anne (John) finds herself (himself) at the top of her (his) medical school class." The women wrote stories about Anne; the men wrote stories about

John. Fear of success was scored if the story mentioned any negative consequences of the success, negative feelings about it, or withdrawal from it. In the original study of ninety females and eighty-eight males at the University of Michigan, 65 percent of the women and only 10 percent of the men showed fear of success.[3] Typical stories scored for fear of success, indicating fear of social rejection or loneliness were the following:

> Anne has a boyfriend, Carl, in the same class, and they are quite serious. Anne met Carl at college, and they started dating about their sophomore year in undergraduate school. Anne is rather upset and so is Carl. She wants him to be higher scholastically than she is. Anne will deliberately lower her academic standing the next term, while she does all she subtly can to help Carl. His grades come up and Anne soon drops out of med school. They marry and he goes on in school while she raises their family.

> Anne is a wonderful girl who has always succeeded. She never had to work. Anne didn't really care. She went to med school because she couldn't marry . . . She really cares nothing about it and wants to get married. No one will marry her. She has lots of friends but no dates. She's just another girl. She tries to pretend intelligence is not part of her. She doesn't hide it—just ignores it. She will get a great job in a marvelous hospital. I don't know if she will ever marry.

> Anne doesn't want to be number one in her class. She feels she shouldn't rank so high because of social reasons. She drops down to ninth in the class and then marries the boy who graduates number one.

Concern over one's normality or feminity also accounted for many stories in which fear of success was scored. For example:

> Anne has planned for a long time to be a doctor. She has worked hard in her schoolwork to enable her to learn better how to fulfill her dream. Now her hard work has paid off. Unfortunately, Anne suddenly no

longer feels so certain that she really wants to be a doctor. She wonders if perhaps this isn't normal . . . Anne decides not to continue with her medical work but to continue with courses that she never allowed herself to take before but that have a deeper personal meaning for her.

Anne cannot help but be pleased; yet she is unhappy. She had not wanted to be a doctor . . she had half hoped her grades would be too poor to continue, but she had been too proud to allow that to happen. She had worked extraordinarily hard and her grades showed it. "It is not enough," Anne thinks. "I am not happy." She is not sure what she wants—only feels the pressure to achieve something, even if it's something she doesn't want. Anne says "To hell with the whole business" and goes into social work—not hardly as glamorous, prestigious, or lucrative; but she is happy.

Finally, in some stories reality was seriously denied or distorted, or disbelieved. The following are typical of stories in this category:

Anne is a *code* name for a nonexistent person created by a group of med students. They take turns taking exams and writing papers for Anne . . .

Anne is talking to her counselor. The counselor says she will make a fine nurse. She will continue her med school courses. She will study very hard and find she can and will become a good nurse.

It was luck that Anne came out on top of her med class because she didn't want to go to med school anyway.

Horner's studies indicate that only women of high ability, who could reasonably expect to be successful, are likely to show fear of success. She found more fear of success among honors students. Women students with fear of success tended to be planning careers in traditional fields for women (such as teaching, nursing, and social work), or they shifted to these fields in the course of their four years at college. Those without fear of success were more likely to be headed for fields traditionally dominated by men (such as law, medicine, and engineering). Women with fear of success performed more poorly at intellectual tasks when competing with persons of the opposite sex than they did in a noncompetitive situation. Those without fear of success performed better in a competitive situation, as do male students.

Considering the expectations (or nonexpectations) about ourselves which most women have, our conflicts about success, and the very practical obstacles most of us have faced, the surprising fact is not that so few women have been successful—but that *any* have. Virginia Woolf speculated in her insightful and penetrating essay, *A Room of One's Own*, published in 1929, on what would have been the fate of the wonderfully gifted sister of Shakespeare, if he had had one. She concluded that "any woman born with a great gift in the sixteenth century would certainly have gone crazed, shot herself, or ended her days in some lonely cottage outside the village, half witch, half wizard, feared and mocked at." Surveying the women of literature, Virginia Woolf mused on what the four most famous women novelists—George Eliot, Jane Austen, Emily and Charlotte Bronte—had in common. Her summary: none of them had children, they wrote only novels, and their freedom of movement was so restricted "that all those good novels, *Villette, Emma, Wuthering Heights, Middlemarch,* were written by women without more experience of life than could enter the house of a respectable clergyman."

There are some barriers to success in women which are so subtle that few people are even aware of them. The personality traits which are generally considered desirable in women are the very opposite of those needed for success in the world. Not long ago a group of social scientists investigated clinical judgments of the traits characterizing healthy, mature people.[4] They expected to find that there was one set of standards for healthy men, another for healthy women. They gave seventy-nine clinical psychologists, psychiatrists, and social workers (forty-six men and thirty-three women) three rating sheets listing paired extremes of behavior. They were asked to indicate on one sheet which traits were socially desirable for mature, healthy, socially competent males. On a second they were to select the traits which best represented mature, healthy, socially competent females, and on a third to choose those characteristic of mature, healthy, socially competent adults (sex unspecified).

The results provided clear evidence that these clinicians had a double standard of mental health. They described healthy women as more submissive, less independent, less adventurous, more easily influenced, less aggressive, less competitive, more excitable in minor crises, having their feelings more easily hurt, being more emotional, more concerned about their appearance, less objective, and disliking math and science. When asked to describe a healthy adult, sex not specified, they chose the characteristics they had ascribed to men. The judgments of these mental health professionals seemed to clearly reflect the cultural stereotypes of our society. Because of the influences exerted by psychiatrists and psychologists, the findings of this study are particularly upsetting. But they are not surprising.

Research into the family backgrounds and personality characteristics of successful women is a very recent development. Many facets remain to be investigated. But the findings of studies which have already been published are remarkably consistent. They indicate that successful women do in fact have the characteristics most commonly associated with healthy, adult men. Their parents have brought them up to be independent and achievement-oriented. Most often they have had a successful woman to identify with as well as a father who encouraged them to think that all possibilities were open to them, regardless of their sex, and who at the same time accepted them as girls.

2

A Forecast of Your Daughter's Life

By looking at the facts about women and work today, you can form some reasonable expectations about the likelihood of your daughter's participation in the labor force.

The chances are that she will be working.

More than half the women of America in the eighteen to sixty-four age bracket (56.9 percent) were in the labor force in 1977. The median age of women workers was thirty-five years, and labor force participation was highest among women twenty to twenty-four years of age with 66.5 percent employed. Fifty-seven percent of the women working in March 1976 were married and almost two out of five had children under eighteen years of age. Of all married women living with their husbands, 57 percent were working.[1]

According to the U.S. Department of Labor, nine out of ten women will work outside the home at some time in

11

their lives. Since some (but not all) women leave the labor force when children are born, returning to it later, the work life expectancy of the average woman worker in 1974 was twenty-five years, compared to forty-three years for men. An increasing proportion of young married women with and without children are remaining in the labor force. Fifty-two percent of married women twenty-five to thirty-four years of age were working in March 1977, compared with fewer than three out of ten in 1963 and two out of ten in 1948.

During the last three decades a dramatic rise has occurred in the overall employment of women. In 1940, 26 percent of women were working. By 1960 the figure had risen to 35 percent and by 1977 to 57 percent. In all, more than 39 million women were in the labor force.

The more education a woman has, the more likely she is to be among those employed. In 1977, 62 percent of women with four years of college were in the labor force. Of those with five or more years of college, 72 percent—almost three out of four—were working. Approximately four out of five women with doctorates are currently working in their professional fields, and of these two-thirds are working full time. In a recent study of the wives of M.I.T. graduates, the only women with professional qualifications who were not working were those with preschool children at home.[2] Half of those with preschool children were working.

Since just before World War II, while the percentage of employed women has doubled, the percentage of working mothers has increased much more dramatically. In 1977, five out of ten mothers (of children under 18) were working, compared to three out of ten in 1960 and less than one out of ten in 1940. More than one out of three of these working mothers had children under six years of age.

Among married women living with their husbands,

one-third of the mothers with children under six years of age, and half of those with school age children only were workers. However, among widows, divorcees, and women separated from their husbands, more than half of those with preschool children and two-thirds of those with school age children only were working. In general, employed mothers are likely to have more education than are other employed women.

The employment of women with children has been accused of causing all kinds of ill effects on their children, including juvenile delinquency. Most American women continue to want to be with their children when they are young, at least part of the time. But not a shred of research evidence has been produced which shows any negative effects of the mother's working.

One study, which compared working mothers of elementary school children who liked their work with those who didn't, found that mothers who liked their work tended to feel guilty about it and to compensate by being overindulgent.[3] Their children actually helped less around the house than children of nonworking mothers. They also seemed less likely to initiate interaction with their peers and to be somewhat underachieving at school. The pattern was not extreme, and it was not found in children of high school age. The effect appeared due not to employment itself but to guilt about it.

Of course, making arrangements for suitable child care is of the utmost importance when a mother works. According to the Department of Labor, more than half the children under twelve years of age whose mothers were working in 1974 were cared for in their own homes, with about a fourth being cared for in someone else's home.[4] Group arrangements, such as day-care centers, accounted for only a small percentage. If mothers are going to continue to work in ever increasing numbers, which seems likely to be the case, it is vital that more attention be given to the provision of high quality child care centers.

Elizabeth Janeway, among others, has recently urged businesses to take the initiative in setting up day care centers where their employees could bring their children and be with them during lunch hours and other routine breaks.[5] Such arrangements would enable many more women to continue working when their children are young and could also provide enriching and educational experiences for the children. I suspect that if such centers are to emerge, the initiative for bringing them about will have to be taken, in most cases, by women.

While there are no measurable ill effects of maternal employment on the children, the effect on the mother varies. One major community mental health study found that in the lower and lower-middle socioeconomic classes, working mothers exhibited better mental health than did nonworking mothers. In the higher socioeconomic classes, however, the same study found nonworking mothers in slightly better mental health.[6] Here again it is probably the guilt about employment, not the employment *per se*, which is causing the problem.

There may also be consequences of *not* working, especially for women with professional training and experience. In a study of forty-six middle-class mothers, "extensive" or "severe" crisis reactions following birth of their first child were reported by 83 percent—and by all of those with extensive professional training and work experience.[7] More recently, a comparison of married career women, single career women, and housewives, all of whom had been high achievers in college, found the housewives very low in self-esteem.[8]

In any case, it seems likely that your daughter is going to be working for at least twenty-five years of her life. The level of work she aspires to, and the seriousness of purpose with which she approaches it, will be partially a function of the kind of early experience and training she receives at home. If she plans a professional career it will be important for her to work continuously, even if she chooses to work part-time for a few years. The interrupted career is not conducive to high level accomplishment in scientific fields or in most other demanding professions. In fact, in all but the most menial of occupations, the interrupted career pattern almost guarantees lower earnings and less responsible work.

Despite the increasing participation of women in the labor force, there has not been a corresponding increase of women in top level occupations. On the contrary, there has been a slight but definite decline since 1940 in the proportions of professional, technical, and kindred positions held by women.[9] Women earned a smaller percentage of the doctorates awarded in 1970 than they did in 1930. There has been an increase in the absolute number of women in professional occupations, but the percentage increase in most cases is less than that for men.

Greater percentages of increase for women did occur, between 1960 and 1970, in a few specific professions that already had an overwhelming majority of men, such as auditors and accountants, physicians and surgeons, and architects. The number of males employed as architects increased 47 percent, while women in this field increased 125 percent. But the percentage of women in the architectural field increased only from 2 percent in 1960 to 3.5 percent in 1970. The number of women veterinarians tripled during this decade (bringing their total number to 989) but their overall percentage in the profession rose only from 2 to 5 percent. In engineering, where slightly more than 1 percent of those professionally employed were women in 1950, there was a rise to slightly more than 2 percent in 1960 and a drop to less than 2 percent in 1970. This occurred despite a rise in the absolute number of women employed in every branch of engineering.

Women's annual earnings also continue to be substantially lower than those of men. This is true even when only full-time workers are considered. In recent years, the gap between men's and women's earnings has been widening.

In the professional and technical category, full-time women workers continue to earn consistently less than men. In 1977, the median income for women in this category was $11, 072, compared to $16, 939 for men.[10]

Because some of the wage differential between the sexes is due to the fact that women have generally had less work experience than men, a study was undertaken a few years ago comparing the incomes of men aged thirty to forty-four with the incomes of women in the same age category who were similar in education, occupational status, and work experience. The women in this study had all worked for at least six months of every year since leaving school. Even with age, experience, and occupational status held constant, men earned an average of $2,800 more than did women. While there was a definite relationship between income and educational level, women's incomes tended to cluster in the average range, while the men's were skewed toward higher income levels.[11]

Given these facts about women's employment, is it possible to make any predictions about the years ahead? Projections for 1970–2000 show a continued rise in the demand for female labor, despite the current recession and higher levels of unemployment.[12] These demands are likely to be concentrated in the occupations in which women are already overrepresented, although legislation against job discrimination should make it increasingly possible for women to enter fields which have been dominated by men. Projections of supply and demand also indicate that older and married women are in the job market to stay. In addition, as more and more women of all ages continue to enter the labor force, continuous career patterns become more and more likely for women. In other words, we have passed the point of no return as far as the employment of women is concerned.

Yet with all of this, the majority of American women continue to be more *job* than *career* oriented. The majority still enter those occupations where part-time work, and less than full commitment, are possible. In some fields, such as engineering or the natural sciences, there are very few women working part time (except in educational institutions), but even here a difference is reported; men are much more likely to be working overtime than are women. Why do women tend to settle for low-status, low-paying jobs? Is it because they fear success and do not want responsibility? Is it because they do not expect work to be important in their lives, so fail to prepare for it? Is it because they are still adhering to outdated societal expectations? Or is it perhaps because their early training and experience have led them to believe women's place is in the home?

Those women who do choose to enter demanding, high level professions may choose not to marry, or they may marry late. The proportion of women who are married declines with each educational level above the bachelor's degree. When women who had received doctorates in 1957–58 were studied several years later, at a time when many were in their forties, only 55 percent were married. In contrast, 80 percent of men with doctorates are married.[13] It is not difficult to understand why this should be so. It is culturally acceptable for men to marry women who are their social or educational inferiors, but few men will marry women they consider their superiors. Therefore, some women at the top are going to be left out.

Even those professional women who do marry have a different attitude about marriage. In a study of twenty families in which the wife as well as the husband was pursuing a serious career, the women were found to be less oriented toward marriage than most other women.[14] Most did marry in their twenties, but early marriage was not their sole preoccupation. One woman described giving up an early relationship because the man was not sympathetic to her career goals.

Small families also characterized this group of professional women. Most of them had from none to two children. Most were in their late twenties when they had their first child, and several were past thirty-five.

Like most women, those in this group of dual-career families had moved at least once because of career requirements of their husbands. But, unlike most men, the majority of the husbands in the group had also moved at least once because of the wife's career needs. Many other departures from traditional patterns occurred. The husbands actively helped with housework and child care. Few of the wives entertained extensively, even though the husband's position might seem to require it, and many often traveled alone in connection with their work. In almost all of the families the husband was highly supportive of his wife's career.

Other studies have also found that the support and encouragement of the husband is a vital factor in a wife's ability to succeed in a high-level position. My own research findings suggest that *only* if the husband is an active support and help can a married professional woman function in her work without feelings of guilt or conflict. I asked over two hundred Wellesley graduates to write stories in response to four verbal cues, such as the following: "At the end of the day, Joan is staying on at the law firm to complete some work." In the forty-eight stories describing the woman in this cue as a married lawyer with children, a majority made some mention of the guilt or conflict she felt about working. Of those who did not mention such feelings, twelve out of fourteen made specific reference to the husband's help and encouragement.

The fact that married women in professional occupations have supportive, encouraging husbands is no accident. For if such a woman marries she must make certain that her husband will be sympathetic to her career goals and will be willing to live in a different way than he would if she were a housewife. If more women are to pursue serious careers in the future, they must insist on this kind of flexibility and cooperation when they marry.

In the few fields for which information is available, professional women appear likely to marry men in their own or related fields. Among women with professional degrees in engineering, more than half are married to engineers or scientists. Similarly, more than half of women in medicine have husbands in medicine or related fields, and these women almost unanimously stress the support their husbands gave them in completing their training and continuing their work after marriage.

3

Avoiding Sexual Stereotypes

Very early in life, children develop expectations about what is appropriate behavior for girls, and what is appropriate for boys.

The process by which these ideas are acquired primarily involves observation of and identification with parents, as well as the learning that occurs through direct parental teaching. The parent responds with pleasure to some of the child's actions, and with displeasure to others. In this way the child learns what is expected. A female child learns what is expected for girls—and equally important, what is *not* expected. We call the process "sex-typing."

Sex-typing begins at birth. Recently a group of investigators at Tufts University turned up evidence suggesting that the process begins with the statement, "It's a girl." Thirty pairs of parents of first born children were interviewed within twenty-four hours of the birth of their first child. They were asked to complete a questionnaire which rated the baby on eighteen adjective scales such as firm-soft, big-little, relaxed-nervous, cuddly-not cuddly, excitable-calm, and so forth. Although objective data from hospital records of weight, height, and Apgar scores (a doctor's ratings of certain physical and activity variables) showed no real differences between the fifteen male and fifteen female infants, both mothers and fathers of girls described their babies as softer, finer featured, smaller, and more inattentive than did parents of boys. The fathers went even further, being more extreme in their ratings of both sons and daughters than were mothers. Sons were rated more alert, stronger, and hardier, while girls were said to be more awkward, weaker, and more delicate. Fathers also called their daughters "cuddlier," while mothers said sons were cuddlier. Investigators dubbed this the "Oedipal effect."[1]

Not only do parents regard male and female infants differently, they treat them differently too. Female infants are usually dressed in pink, while blue is reserved for males. Parents are generally very careful not to put pink on male babies, or blue on females, although they may use neutral colors—usually yellow—for either. Even for infants, toy selections are likely to differ according to the sex of the baby. Physical play is usually rougher with male infants; parents tend to handle female children more delicately and speak to them more softly. Parents are more apprehensive about the physical well-being of females than males. All of this is setting the stage for the perpetuation of sexual stereotypes which are so handicapping to women in later life. If we want more women to enter scientific fields and other occupations, major changes in our methods of child rearing will have to occur. This is equally true if more women are to engage in sports competition, become electricians or plumbers,

or successfully manage their own businesses. Our current child rearing patterns are, for the most part,
designed to maintain the *status quo* as far as life planning for women is concerned.

Like many areas of human behavior, the subject of sex
differences is full of conflict about which part of the difference is due to heredity and which part to environment. There is no simple answer to this problem. Some
of the differences between the sexes are probably biologically determined, but certainly not all of those that
commonly occur. Our methods of bringing up children
maximize, rather than minimize, these differences.

Observations of newborns in hospital nurseries indicate that some definite personality traits are present at
birth. Some babies, for example, are "born difficult."
These children are active and irritable, crying more frequently and demanding the attention of whoever is present. Other infants are passive and compliant. In a recent
study of thirty first born infants and their mothers, some
definite differences were found along sex lines.[2] Males
averaged less sleep and more crying than females at the
age of three weeks and again at three months. Probably
as a result of their increased wakefulness and activity, the
males received more attention from their mothers than
did the females. By the age of three months, while males
were still crying more and receiving more attention, an
interesting difference had developed. The more irritable
male babies were receiving less attention than the less
irritable male babies, while the more irritable female
babies continued to receive more attention from the
mothers. It appeared that either the mothers had learned
that they could not easily soothe an upset male child, or
had classified this behavior as typically masculine.

While there were apparently some differences be-tween
the infants from the beginning, with more of the males

being irritable than the females, the mothers' differential responses to their cries tended to increase these differences. This is what happens continually in the process of bringing up children. Every day, parents reinforce
the behaviors they consider sex-appropriate and the child
gradually internalizes these concepts.

It is important for you as parents to become aware of
what behaviors you may have unwittingly been reinforcing. A smile, a kiss, a pat on the head—these are
powerful reinforcers, and children quickly learn how to
obtain them. Little girls who sit quietly and demurely
like good children, and receive praise for doing so, will
continue this behavior. Telling a child how pretty she
looks is certainly a natural thing to do at times, but its
frequent repetition stresses to her that a pretty appearance is what is important. We all have a natural inclination to treat girls and boys differently, and, as I have
already pointed out, this only serves to increase the differences between the sexes.

In another recent study of sixty-four infants at six
months of age, mothers of girls touched their infants
more than mothers of boys, and they talked more to the
girls. When studied again at thirteen months of age,
these same girls were much more reluctant to leave their
mothers, on being removed from their laps, than were the
boys. Once they left their mothers' laps, girls returned
more often to touch their mothers, looked at them more
frequently, and talked to them more. When the infants
were separated from their mothers by a mesh barrier, the
girls consistently cried and motioned for help more than
the boys. Boys spent more time actively trying to get
around the barrier. There was a definite relationship
between the amount of physical contact the mother made
with a child at six months and the child's behavior at
thirteen months. The more physical contact the mother

made with a boy at six months, the more he touched her at thirteen months. For girls, the relationship was a little different. Those who had received either very much or very little physical contact at six months were more likely to seek a great deal of contact with the mother at thirteen months.[3]

It seems obvious from these results that what parents do actively influences the development of sex-role behavior within the first year of life.

When a comparison of toy preference was made among the same group of children, the investigators found that girls and boys made similar selections. But girls made more choices involving fine muscle coordination (blocks, stuffed dog, and stuffed cat), while boys selected more toys involving gross motor coordination (mallet and lawnmower). The boys' manner of play was more vigorous. While girls tended to sit and play with toys, boys banged them.

Of course, most parents expect such differences in toy preference and in the kind of play evidenced by girls and boys. They tend to reward the girl with a smile and a pat on the head while she sits demurely with a stuffed animal. And they smile encouragingly or verbally approve a boy for vigorously pushing a toy lawnmower.

Researchers at West Virginia University investigated parental effect on toy preference when they asked a group of young mothers, all of whom had young children of both sexes, to play with a six-month old infant. The same infant was presented to each mother, but half of them saw the baby dressed in blue pants and were told that his name was Adam, while the other half saw the baby in a pink dress and were introduced to her as Beth. Three toys, a doll, a fish, and a train, were available in each situation. Mothers presented the doll more often to Beth than to Adam, and the train more often to Adam.

However, when interviewed after the experiment, all mothers insisted that they do not treat their male and female children differently.[4]

These differences in parental action and reaction make it impossible to determine how much of the male-female difference is biological and how much is environmental. Clearly, some sex-typing has occurred by the time a child is a few months old, and probably even sooner.

In an investigation of toy preference in older children, 300 children were asked to choose from a group of sixteen toys—eight commonly associated with girls, eight commonly associated with boys. The boys showed clear cut patterns of preference at an earlier age than girls. Strong patterns of preference also occurred earlier among lower-class children than among middle-class children.[5] Among the lower socioeconomic groups, ideas about appropriate behavior for males and females are stronger and are established earlier. Middle-class mothers seldom limit female children to feminine toys or deliberately inhibit tomboy behavior. Such girls who demand tricycles and trains usually get them. However, unless the child is aggressive or assertive enough to insist on these items they are not necessarily offered to her.

Probably because of their generally limited exposure to typically masculine activities, most middle-class girls are relatively preoccupied with domestically oriented toys during the preschool years. Their interest in dolls, toy dishes, ironing boards, and the like reaches a peak at about age five. After this age other activities such as skating, jumping rope, and playing with jacks become a part of the typical girl's behavior repertoire. However, even at age eight a wide range of domestic activities (helping hang up clothes, caring for a baby, going to get groceries) is seen as appropriate for girls but not for boys. By the age of eleven, most activities considered appropriate for boys but not for girls were avoided by the majority of girls studied. Thus in the early school years there appears to be first a broadening, then a restricting, of the range of middle-class girls' activities and interests.

In another technique for measuring sex-role preferences, the *It Scale*, girls and boys are asked to indicate from pictures of objects commonly associated with one sex or the other (toys, clothes, games) which they would choose for a sexless figure, designated as "It." Studies of children of kindergarten through fifth grade have shown that definite sex-role preferences exist at all ages for both boys and girls.[6]

Boys grow increasingly more masculine in their preference scores as they grow older, and girls' preferences also become slightly more masculine-oriented. At all ages, girls' preference scores are more variable than boys. Preschool girls show the most typically feminine sex-role preferences of any group of girls in the three to ten age period.

Many of these preferences simply reflect what toys children are used to. One of the things you can most easily do as a parent to avoid sex role stereotyping is to avoid toys which perpetuate traditional images. Girls can still have dolls and toy dishes—but their brothers should play with these too. Girls should also have equal opportunity to play with erector sets, tools, fire trucks, doctor's kits, and scientific toys. But old ideas die hard. *Ms.* magazine reported in 1972 that in thirty hours of Christmas time observation in a toy department, no field worker reported a single scientific toy bought for a girl.

Actually, most toys are bisexual and can be enjoyed by both boys and girls. But the packaging is often sexist. A chemistry set picturing a boy on the cover and a set of dishes portraying an apron-clad girl can give a salient message to a child. Even the toys which show both sexes on the cover are likely to show a boy actively doing something, while a girl looks on admiringly. If no tool box or

fishing rod can be purchased without offensive packaging, then the package should be removed and the toy
rewrapped in plain paper.

In general, the most successful toys, those which are
the most fun and last the longest, are those allowing for
unstructured play. Hardwood building blocks, art materials, record players, nature kits, kites, roller skates,
wagons, bicycles, field glasses, microscopes, tents, and
tools are conductive to happy experimentation and play
by children of both sexes.

When you are choosing books for your daughter, it is
also important to avoid those which perpetuate existing
sex role stereotypes. Look for books in which intelligence
and courage pay off for females as well as males. A classic
which meets this prescription is *The Wizard of Oz.*
Others are *Pippi Longstocking* by Astrid Lingren, *Harriet the Spy* by Louise Fitzhugh, and *Island of the Blue
Dolphins* by Scott O'Dell. For preschool children, some
good beginnings are *Madeline's Rescue* by Ludwig
Bemelmans, *Mommies at Work* by Eve Merriam, and
Girls Can Be Anything by Roy Doty. *True Grit* by
Charles Portis and *Daughter of Discontent* by Hila
Coleman are two of the books which can be recom-
mended for girls aged twelve or more. Biographies and
autobiographies of famous women are also must reading
for your daughter.

An important rule to follow is: read the book yourself
before giving it to your daughter. (Of course, I am talking about very young daughters now, since older ones
will be choosing their own books.) Avoid books which
reinforce existing stereotypes and portray girls and
women in passive, dependent roles.

Much of the prevailing advice to parents, like some of
the books on the market for children, serves to perpetuate traditional preferences and prejudices. Dr. Benjamin
Spock, probably still the most widely read authority on

child raising, advises fathers to show their appreciation of a daughter and a girl "with a warm compliment when she has baked a cake or has got herself up prettily, by enjoying the story she tells him, by playing a table game with her after having been away somewhere with her brother."[7] Nowhere do we find Dr. Spock suggesting that "she" could have gone along—but that is exactly what *I* am suggesting.

Dr. Spock is worried that fathers who really wanted a son will show their approval of their daughter mainly when she is acting like a boy. While he doesn't specify exactly what he means by this, he comments that "we see how hard it is for such a girl as she grows up to get satisfaction from most of the jobs (including wifehood) that women have." Dr. Spock is obviously a member of the old school, and I am afraid that his view of women's role is still a rather popular one.

More than a century and a half ago, the feminist Elizabeth Cady Stanton tried to please her father by learning Greek and horseback riding. While grieving over the death of his only son, in 1826, her father said, "Oh, my daughter, I wish you were a boy!"[8] She subsequently attempted to prove herself as good as a boy by emulating the accomplishments which had distinguished her dead brother from herself and her sisters. But apparently her father was not satisfied.

Sometimes fathers do encourage their daughters in just the kind of accomplishment—"acting like a boy"— which Elizabeth Cady Stanton's father could not accept in a girl and which, a century and a half later, Dr. Spock is still worried about.

Dr. Spock is not the only one who is concerned about this, of course. A National Opinion Research Center survey of 1961 college graduates indicates that this factor operates to prevent women's choice of certain occupations, primarily engineering. These women college graduates indicated that primary reasons for not choosing medicine or science as a career were the difficulty of combining demanding professional work with family responsibilities and the difficulty of obtaining part-time work. There was little tendency to consider medicine or science as "unfeminine" or to believe that women lacked the necessary talents to succeed in them. However, different reasons were given for not choosing engineering as a career. The respondents felt that they would be considered unfeminine if they entered the engineering field, and also reported that their parents discouraged them from entering it and that the profession requires skills and characteristics which women do not have.[9] It seems that a childhood of learning appropriate sex role behavior effectively prevents girls from developing interests which might lead to careers in engineering or even from considering themselves competent to enter the field.

There is some indication that these stereotypes are gradually weakening. At UCLA, for example, 153 or 7.4 percent of the 2,075 engineering students enrolled at the beginning of 1975 were women.[10]

Women in the same NORC survey also reported that they felt their mothers and most women would disapprove of women engineers even more than of women business executives. But they felt that their husbands, fathers, and most men disapproved more of women business executives. This perception is probably accurate, for there is a kind of ingrained reluctance on the part of many men to permit women to exercise authority over them.

The available evidence indicates that the one situation in which women are most likely to acquire the inclination and capacity for exercising authority is in a family where there are no sons.

Recently a study was made of twenty-five women presidents and vice presidents of medium to large, nationally recognized business firms, all with direct influence over major decision and policy making. This study is particularly important because when it was done, in 1968, only 100 women in the entire United States held such positions. The investigator found that all twenty-five women were only children or the first born *in an all girl family*. All had warm, close relationships with both parents but reported an atypically warm, supporting, and sharing relationship with the father.

These women had, as children, shared their fathers' personal interests, activities, and enthusiasms—much as a son might have done. The fathers participated with their daughters in frequent male activities, supporting their daughters as females yet demanding that they engage in many activities and engage in competition with both girls and boys.

When this unusual group of women began school, they were unaware that sex-related taboos existed. Their first year in school tended to be an upsetting one. Their behaviors were not the passive, ladylike ones that the teachers expected, but their parents supported their right to act in this atypical manner and tried to change the teachers' attitudes about appropriate behavior for girls.[11]

As I have said before, research into the factors which produce successful women is only beginning, but there is plenty of evidence already that sex-typed behavior is, at least to a large extent, learned.

Avoiding sex-role stereotypes does *not* mean avoiding close, warm physical contact with children of either sex. All children, male as well as female, require such love and contact if they are to develop properly and be able to form loving relationships as adults.

4

Building Self-Confidence

I was greatly impressed by a statement I recently read by a woman who attributed her professional success to her father, explaining that "he made me feel I could do anything."

After thinking this over I realized that to a large extent I also received the same message from *my* father, and that I have tried to pass it along to my own children.

It is particularly important to instill a feeling of self-confidence in your daughter during her early years, because she is likely to have many experiences later which will cause her to wonder if she is inferior to men. Most women learn early in life that they have a different destiny, and in many respects a lesser one, than men. This cultural expectation is certain to undermine self-confidence in women, and without self-confidence it is virtually impossible for anyone, male or female, to accomplish anything of significance.

During several years when I worked with troubled adolescent girls, many of whom had suffered extreme deprivation at home, I daily saw feelings of worthlessness and inadequacy so profound that they were literally irreversible. Such young people have an overwhelming sense of helplessness about themselves and their futures. They have had no experience of success or acceptance in the past, and envision none in the future. It is no wonder that such children fail. They expect failure and unconsciously behave in such a manner that it is certain to occur.

Working with adolescents who have experienced the pain of neglect and rejection is a challenge, for if they are to become whole they must gradually integrate the idea that they are not "bad," that they do have positive qualities, and that they are capable of succeeding. These changes in self-concept occur very slowly—if indeed they can be brought about at all.

The knowledge that a therapist or other staff member sincerely likes her may instill the first ray of hope into the life of a child who has known only rejection. Such a child must be helped to accomplish small things before she can tackle major areas. Being able to read one book, learning to crochet, or getting through a day at school without incurring the teacher's displeasure may be an important step toward self-confidence after a long history of failure.

In middle-class families, it is likely to be rejection in a more subtle form or pushing a child beyond her capacities which poses the greatest threat to a developing self-esteem. An exaggerated idea of a child's abilities, coupled with a lack of understanding of the limits which are more or less determined by heredity, can cause a parent to err in this direction.

While interning in a psychiatric hospital, I had as a patient, a young black girl, who had suffered a psychotic break during a hopeless struggle to complete an engineering program at a competitive university. Neither the girl nor her father could accept the fact that her educational goals were not appropriate for her, and her mother, who did understand, was powerless to intervene. The father, himself an engineer who owed his social position to his profession, saw no reason why his daughter could not succeed in the same field if she worked hard—as he had.

It is unusual for unrealistic parental expectations to have consequences as dire as these, but many children do suffer from being pushed beyond their abilities. In the long run such prodding is harmful to the child's self-concept, for she repeatedly fails as she attempts to achieve impossible goals.

Unfavorable comparisons with an older, brighter or more accomplished sibling can be devastating to a child's self-esteem. A child who is continually told she does not live up to an older sister or brother's accomplishments can never take pride in her own, however praiseworthy they may be. I have talked to many women who as children were made to feel they were inferior or second rate compared to an older brother. My closest childhood friend recently (more than thirty years later) told me that *she* had always felt that way.

If a child is to develop self-esteem, she must be esteemed by the people most important in her world— her parents. One of the ways self-esteem is built is through the unconditional love that the young child receives from her parents. In the beginning this love is expressed through physical affection, a warm loving manner, and meeting the child's basic needs. A little girl who grows up in a warm atmosphere where all her needs are met will naturally feel loved and wanted, and this kind of experience is essential to the development of a positive self-concept.

As your child grows older, you also develop self-esteem by responding with warm approval to the positive aspects of her behavior. This doesn't mean criticism should never be offered. All children need to be corrected at times, and it isn't really possible to raise a child using positive reinforcement alone. ("Positive reinforcement" is a term used by behaviorally oriented psychologists to indicate praise and other forms of social or material rewards.)

Many parents, even well-meaning ones, fall into a pattern of responding negatively when a child behaves in an undesirable manner and ignoring the good things she does. Since children all want attention and quickly learn how to get it, noticing only the negatives has the effect of creating more of them. But this negative attention, while it has reinforcing value, doesn't serve to enhance a child's self-concept. In fact, the opposite occurs.

If you make a deliberate effort to look for positive behaviors in your daughter, and to notice and comment on them, you will help her not only to exhibit more of the desirable behaviors but to develop a positive self-concept at the same time. Often you have the opportunity to choose between commenting on the negative or positive aspects of the same performance.

Let's say, for example, that your ten-year-old daugher keeps the family waiting for ten minutes before appearing immaculately dressed for an evening at the movies. It is usually more constructive to praise her for her good-looking outfit than berate her for tardiness. If the tardiness is important and must be mentioned, try to make a positive comment too if one is appropriate.

Constructive criticism is not harmful to a child (or adult) who has a positive self-concept, but the best intentioned suggestion may seem devastating to a child who feels generally inadequate.

Sarcasm and belittling remarks, even when they are

meant to be teasing or humorous, have no place in child rearing. Unfortunately some parents do use such tactics. Often they are repeating patterns they experienced in their own childhood or acting out some deep seated frustrations. "Fumblefingers," "Fats," or "Slowpoke" may seem like accurate descriptions of a child at some stages of her development, but the pain and embarrassment that such labels cause often lingers on in the child's mind for years after everyone else has forgotten that the nickname ever existed.

Many clients who seek psychotherapy have problems concerning self-esteem. They almost always feel inadequate in solving their own problems and often feel inadequate in general. They may feel they are incapable of giving and receiving love. In a successful therapeutic relationship the client gradually alters such beliefs as it becomes clear that the therapist likes and accepts the client despite the negative traits and behaviors which are revealed. With increased experience in successfully resolving problems, one's feelings of inadequacy are slowly replaced with self-confidence. These middle class adult patients are resolving many of the same issues presented by the adolescent girls described earlier in this chapter, although few of them have suffered such devastating childhood experiences and consequently have more resources for future development.

Self-confidence poses a particular problem for women in our society, since females tend to underestimate their performances far more consistently than do men. Boys set higher standards for themselves. Girls are also more likely to change their minds if presented with the discrepant opinions of others. Males feel in control of their own destiny, while females tend to feel less control. Furthermore, both males and females tend to devalue work done by women. In one recent study, a set of articles from different scholarly disciplines was presented to two groups of college women. The articles were identical, but those presented to one group were ascribed to a female author, those presented to the other to a male. Ratings of articles ascribed to women were consistently lower than ratings of those said to be written by men, regardless of the professional fields involved.[1]

I have personally observed the problem of low self-esteem repeatedly among a group of women in whom I have had a particular interest for many years. I am speaking of well-educated, relatively affluent suburban women in their thirties, forties, and fifties who have come seeking counseling because their children have left home or no longer require their exclusive attention.

These women, almost all of whom are college graduates (many of first rate, prestigious colleges) have invariably been full-time housewives. While many have been active in volunteer work and the majority are more or less happily married, it appears that their lack of involvement in the world of work or in some engrossing activity *of their own* has resulted in a drastic loss of self-confidence. The problem is self-perpetuating, for with such low selfesteem it is difficult to take the steps needed to start or resume a career or to become involved in other meaningful activities outside the home.

Even the prospect of facing an interview with an employment agent or the dean of a college may seem like an insurmountable barrier to one who feels incapable of doing anything alone. Not long ago I was asked by an extremely bright acquaintance who dropped out of a Ph.D. program at Harvard because of family responsibilities to help her write a letter to the dean asking if she might resume her work. Her self-confidence had been so undermined by her retirement from intellectual life that she doubted her ability to compose a simple letter.

I have seen few women—though undoubtedly there are

some—who have concentrated their attention solely on their families for extended periods of time and have retained much in the way of self-confidence. It is true, of course, that the women who come to me for counseling are primarily those who are no longer satisfied with the housewife role and are seeking new directions for their lives.

At least two nationwide mental health surveys report that among their married subjects the women are unhappier, have more problems, feel more inadequate as parents, and have a more negative self-image.[2] Alice Rossi, a well-known sociologist, speculates that the personal consequences of marriage and child rearing for women—in contrast to men—is a depressed sense of self-worth and sometimes actual personality deterioration. Rossi believes that the family-oriented woman will experience anxiety and doubt as the nest empties, while the career-oriented woman will be deriving much satisfaction from her work at this stage of life.[3]

In a recent study comparing married professional women, single professional women, and homemakers who showed the same high degree of academic distinction in their undergraduate years, the married professional women were distinguished from the other two groups by the greater self-assurance they recalled having as children and the much higher self-esteem they reported at the time of the study. Thirty-one percent of the homemakers were "poor to average" in self-esteem, compared to 14 percent of the single professionals and only 4 percent of the married professionals. At the other extreme, 54 percent of both married and single professionals rated "good to very good" in self-esteem compared to only 14 percent of the homemakers.[1]

Not only was their overall self-esteem higher, but the married professional women felt more competent in caring for and understanding children than did the homemakers who had been devoting themselves exclusively to this task for most of their adult years. Homemakers rated themselves far more inadequate in social skills than either married or single professionals, and far more inadequate in intellectual ability and work skills. The study left little doubt that for these intellectually gifted women, remaining at home was clearly related to a depressed sense of self-worth.

Why did these homemakers feel so inadequate and unworthy? In contrast to their early success in school and college, they felt "let down" and disappointed. With their children growing up and needing them less, the women in this study had a sense of uselessness which appeared to be not a chronic state but a reaction to the realization that the life role they had chosen for themselves was about to come to an abrupt halt. Many of the women, even though they claimed that they were satisfied with the homemaker's role, also stated that they regretted not having combined a career with marriage, or not having established definite occupational goals at an earlier stage in their lives.

For an intellectually gifted girl, it appears not only that high self-esteem iis a prerequisite for professional accomplishment, but also that professional or occupational accomplishment is much more likely to maintain a high level of self-confidence than is the role of homemaker. From my own counseling experience I believe that there is something about the role of housewife itself which brings about a loss of self-esteem, regardless of the woman's intellectual qualifications.

There has been relatively little research on the effect of marriage on women's values, self-conceptions, and self-esteem. Most often, married and unmarried groups have been compared. One study gave personality tests to girls in high school and several years later ascertained which had married and which had remained single. The single girls were more self-reliant, had a greater sense of personal freedom, showed less tendency to withdraw, were more aggressive socially, and better adjusted emotionally.[5]

These results suggest that those who married early did so out of weakness. Another study of the top 1 percent of a freshman class of women at Michigan State University found that those who married before completing their college program had changed from the personality profile they showed as freshmen. After marriage, they showed less independence, reduced impulse expression, greater submissiveness and conservatism.[6]

I believe that further research will confirm these preliminary findings which suggest that anyone who functions in a role which does not allow her to use all her capacities will suffer a loss of self esteem.

If you want your daughter to feel positively about herself, both as a child and as an adult, you must not only do all you can to build self-esteem during her developing years but must encourage the strong interests and independence which will mitigate against early marriage. (Not against marriage, just *early* marriage.)

5

Developing Independence

It is curious that in a nation where independence and personal freedom represent our very reason for being, little thought has been given to the development of independent behavior in girls and women. This trait, desirable as it is for every living person, has been reserved for males, while females have been expected to be dependent and passive.

In the past, and even today, there has been some reality in this expectation since the woman who chooses to remain at home with her children is—barring highly unusual circumstances such as inherited wealth—in an economically dependent position. This expectation undoubtedly has affected our child-raising norms.

It has been assumed that more girls are clinging, dependent, and seek to remain close to their mothers than are boys, and that most parents begin dependency weaning at an earlier age for boys than for girls. However, the small amount of data on this point does not support the assumption. There has been no clear demonstration that girls are more dependent or that they usually receive more reinforcement for dependency than do boys. Up to the age of four, it appears that restrictions on a child's freedom of movement outside the home are not related to sex. However, a longitudinal study being conducted in England does suggest that by the age of seven clear differences emerge.[1] Girls' whereabouts must be known more often and they are more often accompanied to and from school.

I have already mentioned in an earlier chapter a study of attitudes toward desirable personality characteristics in men and women, which clearly indicated that even among professional psychotherapists (psychiatrists, psychologists, and social workers) there is a double standard of mental health. Well-adjusted adult women are expected to be passive, submissive, and dependent. Desirable traits for men and for "healthy adults, sex not specified," according to these therapists, included independence and dominance.

Granted that many women do display these dependent, passive traits, it is difficult to see how they can be regarded as healthy. In their extreme form they can lead to severe disturbance. It is no accident that two-thirds of the agoraphobic patients (those afraid to go out into public places) who consult psychiatrists and psychologists are women, and that most of them grew up in close-knit, overprotective families. Women who develop this condition have usually been brought up by parents who allowed them absolutely no personal freedom. Often they were so apprehensive about their daughter that they refused to leave her in the care of a baby sitter, even a responsible adult relative, for any length of time. Agoraphobia develops most frequently in young married women who may have achieved a degree of independence while single but became stereotypically feminine after marriage. The typical phobic patient needs help not only with her phobias but with her problems in asserting herself and in learning to function in an adult manner.

Even when dependency does not reach the extreme of agoraphobia, it can be crippling. Recently I heard of a young married woman who is so dependent on her husband that she becomes panic stricken and hysterical if he returns five minutes late from work. The problem reached crisis proportions when he accepted a job requiring considerable traveling, a prospect his wife found intolerable.

Many women who appear to be functioning normally in the role of wife and mother are also handicapped by their feelings of dependency, especially when something happens which forces them to stand alone. Not long ago I met a young women whose husband, a business executive, had just been released after several months of political captivity in a South American country. During this time she returned to the United States with her three children and occupied the family's summer home while waiting to learn what had happened to her husband. Despite the uncertainty of the situation, not knowing whether he was dead or alive, she found the experience to be a positive one. After ten years of a typical, supportive, submissive wifely role, she had learned that she could once again function as an independent adult.

Perhaps I am unduly biased, but I can see *no* advantages to dependency and many disadvantages. Even if your daughter marries and accepts the traditional feminine role, is it sensible for her to become totally dependent on another human being, relinquishing personal freedom and the right to assert herself? This is particularly true in view of current statistics which indicate that approximately one out of three marriages ends in divorce. But even in a lasting marriage there are many unfortunate consequences, both psychological and physical, for the woman who relinquishes her selfhood.

There is relatively little doubt that the dependent, passive, typically feminine woman is more suited for the traditional role of wife in our society, if one's concept of a traditional wife means one who stays at home, defers to her husband's wishes, takes no strong stands of her own, and concentrates on looking pretty and feminine. Such women often appear in a psychotherapist's office, many resembling children more than adults, and needing help with the depressions, phobias, and psychosomatic ills they have developed. A recent informal survey of internists and medical groups in Fairfield County, Connecticut, who serve a patient load of approximately 3300 monthly, indicates that approximately half of these patients are actually suffering from emotional problems and "psychophysical ailments," and that a large majority of these patients are women. Fortunately, the women's movement and economic pressures have combined to create a social climate in which the number of wives filling this limited, traditional role is decreasing. Not only are more women entering the labor force, but more of them are insisting on equality of opportunity and treatment not only at work but at home.

Is the trait of dependency an advantage for women who work in traditional female roles? I don't think so, really. Unquestionably traditionally oriented women are more likely to enter traditional fields for women which extend the nurturing role of the homemaker and mother—teaching, nursing, social work. But the leaders in these fields, the Jane Addamses and the M. Carey Thomases, have been strong pioneer women who fought to overcome the traditional limitations on women. (Interestingly enough, both Jane Addams and M. Carey Thomas first aspired to be physicians.)

Even the rank and file worker in a traditional woman's field will be handicapped and ineffective if she is overly dependent. What kind of nurse would most patients prefer, one capable of independent action or one who can only take orders? And in a business office, a degree of initiative and autonomy is almost essential for success in any position other than the simplest clerical job. It seems paradoxical that an overly dependent woman socialized for the traditional female role may even be handicapped in carrying out some of the functions involved in being a mother.

For the adult woman, then, being dependent appears to have few rewards. The parents of a very dependent child may find her helplessness gratifying and appealing, but this kind of satisfaction is experienced at the child's expense and every possible effort should be made to avoid it.

In the very young child, some aspects of independent behavior have practical value in that they release you, the parent, from performing routine tasks. A two-year-old relieves you or your substitute from the necessity of feeding her when she learns to feed herself. A four-year-old who puts on her own snowsuit saves you the trouble of doing it. A six-year-old who is capable of making her own peanut butter sandwich makes it possible for you, or the baby sitter, to do something else.

Other kinds of independent, assertive behaviors lack this practical value and may often appear to be more of a nuisance than anything else. A child who *insists* on feeding herself at all times as soon as she is able to do so is behaving both independently and assertively—and at times this may be inconvenient. One who constantly darts off to explore her surroundings, moving away from her parents in a strange situation to look at what the children on the other side of the room are doing, is also behaving independently and assertively. Typically these

behaviors involve moving away from parents or the
familiar, to explore the unfamiliar or the unknown.
Some psychologists believe that this urge to explore the
environment can be classified as a basic human drive.

In any case, as a child does explore she gradually increases her understanding and mastery of the world
around her. The native intellectual curiosity that most
children display is at first evidenced by simple explorations such as grasping, handling, and letting go of objects (rattles, for starters), but these explorations all have
something in common. They enable the child to interact
competently and effectively with the environment and to
develop a feeling of mastery and autonomy. Gaining
mastery over the environment is usually a solitary pur-
suit which brings its own reward.

In the beginning, your child will move away only
when you are in sight, but as she gains confidence, your
presence will be less necessary. The critical period for the
development of independence and competence is
between a year and three or four years of age. In other
words, this is the age when independence and competence are most easily learned.

Recently, a group of investigators at Harvard studied
child-rearing practices of parents whose kindergarten
and nursery school children were rated highest (in a
group of 400) on overall competence, compared with
those rated lowest. The competent children excelled in
social and intellectual functioning and in using the resources of the environment to best advantage. These investigators found that clear differences between high and
low competent children developed between the first and
third birthdays. And they found certain clear cut differences between mothers of "A" (competent) children and
mothers of "C" children.

The A mothers talked a great deal to their children,
usually at a level the children could understand. They

demonstrated and explained often, but usually on the children's initiative. The A mothers provided an enriched environment full of interesting things to do and look at. They were seldom perfect housekeepers. They were usually permissive (although they firmly said "No" when necessary), and encouraged their children to explore. They seldom kept their children confined in a crib or playpen. They were usually busy themselves and several had part-time jobs, but gave warm support and interest to their children when approached. They seemed to have high levels of energy and to enjoy being with their young children.[2]

Not surprisingly, the capacity to act independently is of major importance in later life. Psychologist Anne Roe found in her famous study of successful scientists that one of their primary characteristics was extreme independence and a desire to be free of supervision. The scientists in her study were all men, but the assumption here is that successful women scientists have similar personality traits.

This ability to act independently, to solve problems alone, to act on one's own initiative rather than relying on the wishes or directions of others, has also been found to be related to the development of mathematical ability in both boys and girls. Independence training appears to be a necessary prerequisite for analytic thinking, while overprotection actually decreases mathematical ability. This was first demonstrated in a study done in the early forties. In this study, boys who were poor at math were found to have mothers who babied them to such an extent that they were still leading them to school by the hand and still dressing them at the age of ten or eleven. The boys were good in their language work at school— but they were notably poor at math.[3]

In a more recent study at Stanford University, children good at verbal tasks but poor at math or spatial relations were compared with children good at math but relatively poor at verbal tasks. Observations of these children's interactions with their mothers revealed the fact that mothers of the highly verbal girls constantly offered suggestions, praised the children for doing well, and criticized them for performing poorly. Girls who were better at math or spatial tasks were more often left alone to solve the problems themselves.[4]

Children who do well on psychological tests of analytic reasoning ability (the "rod-and-frame test" and the "embedded figures test") have also been found to have experienced a particular kind of early childhood training. Their mothers had given them considerable freedom at an early age and had encouraged them to do things on their own initiative.

In contrast, a group of children who did not display analytic thinking on these tests had mothers who were very protective, would not tolerate self-assertiveness, and talked to them about the dangerous aspects of the environment. Girls who do well on these tests also tend to have stronger identification with their fathers than with their mothers.[5]

Some children show consistent rises in IQ from the preschool years through age ten, while others consistently decline. A comparison of two such groups of children found that those with rising IQs were described as competitive, self-assertive, independent, and dominant in interaction with other children. Those with declining IQs were passive, shy, and dependent. In other words, the children with typically masculine characteristics (whether they were male or female) continued to make intellectual gains throughout early childhood, while those with stereotypically feminine characteristics lost ground.[6]

It seems undeniable from these many findings that a girl who is to grow up into a self-reliant adult woman capable of independent action and high level intellectual functioning must be a tomboy at some stage of her life. What is needed is for more girls to be tomboys and to be tomboys longer. If parents accept and encourage a girl's equal right to be assertive and independent in her early years, they may give her the strength she will need to withstand counterencouragements and pressures later. M. Carey Thomas, the eldest in a family of ten children, who subsequently grew up to be the founder of Bryn Mawr and an early, vigorous feminist, was a tomboy and difficult to manage from early childhood. Her mother, recognizing the value of individual personality, did not attempt to curb Minnie's (her childhood nickname) will. For years Miss Thomas struggled to prove that women were capable of the same intellectual distinction as men, and insisted that the entrance examinations for Bryn Mawr be equally as difficult as those for Harvard.

Independence and self-reliance are traits that *must* be cultivated in women if anything other than mediocre accomplishment is to be expected from the female half of the world's population. Conformity to social rules and a dependence on the wishes and authority of others will not produce women scientists, engineers, doctors, lawyers, or business executives. As I have already pointed out, research evidence does not reveal differing socialization of males and females with respect to independence, yet we know that great differences do exist at the adult level. Why? Perhaps girls must receive *more* independence training than boys as children if this trait is to persist into adulthood.

Maria Mitchell, America's famous astronomer, loved mathematics as a child, was a close companion of her father's, and early assisted him in his astronomical observations from their Nantucket "widow's walk." In later years she credited not only her father's example and her love of mathematics as factors influencing her to devote her life to astronomy, but mentioned her environment also. "In Nantucket people quite generally are in the habit of observing the heavens, and a sextant will be found in almost every house." Mitchell also profited from the example of many Nantucket women, forced by the long absences of their sea-faring husbands to behave independently. One of the greatest of Vassar's teachers, Mitchell urged her students to learn not through rote but through observation. "We cannot accept anything as granted beyond the first mathematical formulae," she told them. "Question everything else." She felt that scientific observation was particularly well suited to women. "Nature made woman an observer," she said. "The schools and schoolbooks have spoiled her. . . . So many of the natural sciences are well fitted for women's power of minute observation that it seems strange that the hammer of the geologist is not seen in her hand or the tin box of the botanist."[7]

These words were spoken in the last quarter of the nineteenth century. Many of Mitchell's students followed her inspiring example, and twenty-five of them were listed in *Who's Who in America*, not only in science but in other fields.

Despite the fervor of the early feminists and the success of a few women scientists like Maria Mitchell, old attitudes are extremely difficult to change. As recently as 1961 a study of women college graduates indicated that the majority saw their future success as tied to a husband's and children's accomplishments. What they most wanted for themselves was "to be the wife of a man who becomes very prominent" or "to be the mother of several highly accomplished children." Nevertheless, when asked what kinds of successful women they most admired, four out of five of these college graduates mentioned women who received literary or artistic awards.[8] The question which remains is why so few of these women sought such goals themselves.

My own research, comparing a class out of Wellesley College twenty-five years with another class out ten years, suggests that far more of the younger women are in fact seeking such goals. Proportionately twice as many women in the younger group had earned doctoral level degrees (M.D., J.D., Ph.D.). But the number is still staggeringly low compared to a class from any comparable men's college where a high proportion of graduates obtain top level professional degrees.

I think that any major change in women's aspirations and accomplishments will have to be preceded by the insistence that young girls learn—perhaps overlearn—independence and initiative.

6

Enhancing Achievement Efforts

Being independent is a necessary factor in achievement.

Another aspect is achievement striving itself. Somewhere along the line a child has to acquire this characteristic if she is going to excel in school, in sports, and other extra-curricular activities, and professionally in later life.

A great deal of effort has been expended by psychologists in the measurement of achievement motivation. Most often projective tests, in which subjects are asked to write stories in response to pictures or verbal cues, are used. However, the majority of studies have employed male subjects. The findings concerning the achievement motive in girls and women have been inconsistent and contradictory. In general, men perform better in a competitive situation, but this is not necessarily true of women. In a mixed-sex competitive situation, women tend to perform more poorly than when they are alone.[1]

As I have mentioned in an earlier chapter, Matina Horner, the president of Radcliffe, believes that women actually fear success. She found that as many as 88 percent of high ability women (in a sample at Radcliffe College) told "fear of success" stories in response to the cue, "At the end of first term finals, Anne finds herself at the top of her class in medical school."[2]

Although differing percentages of "fear of success" have been reported using other samples, similar results were recently obtained at another woman's college with students of similar ability level. At Wellesley, 89 percent of an undergraduate sample tested in 1970 told avoidance stories which implied that "the computer made a mistake," "it was just a fluke," or "she won't be able to keep it up."[3] Apparently, even in these days of increasing women's liberation, the concept of achievement is still perceived by a majority of high ability women to be incompatible with femininity.

When the cue was changed to "After first term finals, Anne finds herself at the top of her class," the percentage of women telling negative stories dropped to about fifty. It seemed that what these high ability students were most anxious about was the prospect of success in a masculine-dominated field.

At Wellesley, the investigation measured the role orientations of students as well as achievement motivation, and found that those high in traditional feminine values were more likely to tell fear of success stories than were women low in traditional feminine values. (The "lows" also made higher grades at Wellesley than did the "highs," although their SAT scores did not differ.) This is consistent with Horner's earlier finding that women without fear of success were more likely to be pursuing traditionally masculine occupations.

In a further experiment with Wellesley undergraduates, subjects were shown a "kitchen" picture of a young woman at an easel, painting a portrait of a child seated in a high chair. Women high in feminine role orientation tended to tell stories which suggested that motherhood must come before personal achievement (she had given up her career, or would do so in the future), or that the painting was only a hobby. The "lows" most frequently told stories which indicated that career, marriage, and motherhood *could* be combined or that they could not and the marriage would eventually break up.

My own studies with two samples of Wellesley graduates suggest that a nontraditional role orientation is a prerequisite to high level professional success. Women high in traditional feminine orientation do not become successful doctors or lawyers. This seems relatively obvious, for such women would have no motivation to do so.

Still, there is a point here which is well worth underscoring, I think. It is this. If more women are to achieve, they will have to be brought up in such a way that they develop a nontraditional expectation of their future role in life. Women with a traditional feminine orientation do not see personal achievement as consistent with the female role: hence their "fear of success" stories.

There is also evidence that direct encouragement of achievement-related behavior in young children tends to produce more achievement orientation in young children.[4] (These studies have almost all been done with white middle-class children, and there is no reason to believe that the results generalize to other populations.) Achievement behavior must, of course, be differentiated from simple grade getting. Individuals with intellectual striving, as opposed to academic achievement striving or grade getting goals, exhibit intellectual curiosity and effort not exclusively related to academic rewards. It is a well-known fact that girls outperform boys in school throughout the early years, but some observers feel that girls seek good grades because they are more compliant and seek the approval of adults. In any case, it does not require a very astute observer to note that the superior performance of girls in the early school years does not carry over into later life.

What does carry over is a more general pattern of achievement behavior (not related solely to academic performance) and independence in those girls who show these qualities early. If such patterns are present in girls during middle childhood and adolescence, they are predictive of adult achievement behavior and independence. And certain early child-rearing practices seem to produce achievement behavior in girls during middle childhood and adolescence.

If you want to stimulate achievement behavior in your daughter, here are some concrete things you can do.

Praise your child when she achieves or performs well, or tries to accomplish tasks requiring skill and effort. Putting a puzzle together, building a tower of blocks, reading a book, solving a problem, learning to swim or ride a bike, or identifying a bird or flower, all are examples of achievement strivings in young children. You should make a positive comment when you observe such efforts, even if your daughter doesn't come to you and seek your approval.

You should also try to provide your child with the kinds of play materials which require achievement efforts—puzzles, blocks, building sets and Tinkertoys, and games of skill. Sports competition, for older children, also spurs a child to strive for excellence. Participating with your child in some activities such as games and sports will help too, but direct interference and assistance in problem solving will not. The child should be encouraged to solve the problem by herself.

Achievement-oriented women also tend to have had mothers who actively tried to accelerate their development and expected them to perform at a high level. The available evidence indicates that to some extent, at least, the pushy mother accomplishes what she sets out to do.

Be warm, but not too warm. Early babying, overprotectiveness, and being overhelpful are related negatively to later achievement behavior. If you encourage your child to seek help with a problem, you are rewarding dependency, which doesn't go along with achievement efforts. Responding too quickly with assistance will not help your child develop the ability to tolerate frustration, and she will be more likely later on to withdraw from a difficult task than continue tackling the problem. By grade school age, girls do show greater tendencies than boys to withdraw from threatening situations and seek adult help, though these differences do not appear in preschool children.

While it may seem to you natural to be extremely warm, affectionate, and accepting toward your daughter in her early years, if you carry these attitudes to an extreme you are setting the stage for a stereotypically feminine, passive personality. Both very high degrees of maternal warmth and high degrees of rejection are associated with low achievement behavior in later life.

Paradoxically, a degree of overprotectiveness does not seem to prevent achievement behavior in boys. Of course, most studies of child-rearing patterns compare parents of boys to other parents of boys, and parents of girls to other parents of girls. In other words, the same amount of protective behavior may be average for a boy but low for a girl.

Studies of responsibility and leadership in women also show that very high degrees of warmth or hostility are associated with low responsibility and leadership. The most effective parental attitude. for the development of these traits appears to be moderate warmth and some punishment.

It seems that for your daughter to become achievement oriented, then, you must be sufficiently affectionate and supportive to provide confidence and a feeling of security—but not so much that she doesn't want to move away from the safety and security you stand for.

Be more permissive than restrictive. Highly restrictive child-raising practices produce children low in achievement aspiration, responsibility, and leadership ability. If you impose many rules on your child, for example, prohibiting such behavior as aggression, sexual exploration, exploration of the environment, and so forth, you will be engendering femininity and passivity. But do not confuse restrictiveness with demands for high levels of performance or mature behavior. Such demands *do* lead to achievement-oriented behavior.

Generally speaking, permissiveness in a context of moderate warmth is related to later achievement behavior.[5] In fact, permissiveness by both parents has been found to be associated with achievement behavior in preschool girls.

Is it possible or desirable to discourage your daughter from seeking to gain love and approval? Most parents, myself included, would probably be reluctant to do so in the extreme, yet some efforts must be made in this direction. There is considerable evidence that girls' achievement strivings are often motivated by a need for social approval rather than for mastery. I think this may be very important, for later these two motives come into conflict and probably this accounts for the fear of suc-

cess shown by so many women. If women are ever to
carry the pattern of high achievement established in the
early school years over to later professional and business
life, it seems clear that we must try to instill in our
daughters a desire to achieve which is independent of
social approval.

7

Providing Role Models

There's a popular children's game that illustrates the way children learn a good deal of what they know about their future roles in life (and, of course, about other things as well). The name of the game is "Simon Says."

And the point it proves is that children are more likely to imitate what they see than to follow verbal directions.

Psychologists agree that while parents do respond differently to boys and girls, these differences are actually smaller than one might suppose—and they are by no means powerful enough to account for the sex-typing that we know does occur.

In other words, you cannot expect that all the problems of sex-typing will be solved by giving a baby doll to Johnny or a doctor kit to Mary—as long as Johnny's father wouldn't be caught in the kitchen under any circumstances while Mary's mother can be found there all day, every day, carrying out the traditional domestic

tasks. Approving a little girl's efforts to be independent
and to achieve will do little to guide her away from the
culturally stereotyped feminine role if she sees her
mother engaged in these, and only these, activities.

Most children naturally identify with the parent of the
same sex. A boy derives knowledge and understanding of
his masculine role through observation and identification with his father, or with another male, and often
participates with his father and other males in male-
oriented activities which reinforce this identification.
Similarly, a girl forms her expectations of her feminine
role through observation and identification with her
mother or with another woman.

What this means is that the best way to produce a
daughter who is motivated to pursue a serious career is to
be pursuing one yourself. The daughters of typically
feminine women who occupy themselves with home,
family, volunteer, and community activities seldom grow
up to be doctors, lawyers, engineers, or college professors, unless some other very potent influence is
present.

One of my college classmates has devoted her entire life
since college to her husband, children, and volunteer
activities of which her husband, a traditionalist,
approves. But because he does not approve of her studying or working, she has avoided conflict and has not
done either, though she is a woman of great ability and
knowledge who would have much to give as a college
teacher. She is quite frustrated with her present life and
has told me she hopes her two young daughters will seek
professional careers for themselves, as she has found her
own lifestyle too confining. For her sake and theirs, I
hope that her wish for them may one day be a reality, but
I expect that they will instead follow in their mother's
footsteps and occupy themselves with traditionally feminine activities. With their upbringing this is what they

will be most suited for, but I doubt whether this role will be appropriate for any intelligent woman in tomorrow's world.

The importance of exposing your child to appropriate models—especially yourself—really cannot be overestimated. Yet I constantly meet other women who overlook this factor. Recently at a seminar on women's changing roles and lifestyles I met a housewife in her fifties who declared herself ideally happy in her domestic role (what she was doing at the workshop is another matter!). She has five daughters and exclaimed proudly that all of them were happily married housewives without serious career interests. "I never influenced them in any way," she announced. "I always told them they were free to choose their own way."

But choices are of course made on the basis of known alternatives. A young girl who knows no career-oriented women is quite likely to consider them deviant and unfeminine. In one major study of adolescent females, the majority of those high in traditional feminine interests and low in achievement aspirations said that their mothers and other female relatives were their models. Women with high achievement aspirations, whether or not they also were high in feminine interests, more often named nonfamily models.[1] When such women do say that they modeled themselves after their own mothers, their mothers are likely to be achievement-oriented women with serious career interests of their own.

Not surprisingly, other studies have found the mother's employment in middle-class families to be associated with high educational and occupational aspirations in their daughters. Maternal employment also favorably affects judgments of female competence. Girls with employed mothers tend to see women as more competent than do girls whose mothers are housewives.

Even more significant is the fact that daughters of

working mothers are actually more likely to establish careers and to enter masculine-oriented occupations. When the mother herself is in a masculine-oriented occupation, this is even more true. If you are a physician yourself, naturally your daughter will grow up assuming that this kind of professional activity is compatible with being a woman.

This is the case not only in America but elsewhere in the world. A study done in Israel in 1965 found that women with mothers in high-status positions tended to follow their example, especially if the mothers were in masculine occupations.[2] And in a recent survey of honors graduates of a large middle-western university comparing homemakers, married professionals, and single professionals, far more (36 percent) of the married professionals had mothers who worked regularly for pay, even when their daughters were under five, than did either of the other two groups.[3] More of these mothers also went back to work later than did the other mothers. By the time their daughters reached adolescence, more than half the married professionals' mothers were working outside the home.

Career-oriented women often describe their backgrounds in such terms as:

> All of the women in my family worked. It was expected that I would. Both of my parents were professionals and this influenced my choice to take up a professional occupation.

> I know I am going to work. I enjoy it. I was probably influenced by my mother. She has worked the whole time, except when I was very small.

If the mother was not employed, career-oriented women often report an investment in the values of working:

> My mother was a musician and, primarily out of personal interest, worked part-time as a church organist

until I was about twelve, when an arthritic condition prevented her from continuing. She always encouraged my interest in working, and it was taken for granted that I would have a career.

My mother had taught history in high school before her marriage and in college after World War II to help out in an inflated enrollment situation. Other relatives, including my maternal grandmother, an uncle, and a cousin, had also earned graduate degrees and engaged in college teaching. My parents took it for granted that I would get all the education I was entitled to by virtue of my abilities and then put it to work.[4]

In the background of many famous women there is a working mother, or one with work or intellectual-oriented values—a mother who served as a model for her daughter's future achievement. Margaret Mead writes in her autobiography, *Blackberry Winter*: "From the time I can first remember, I knew that we had not always lived where we were living then—in Hammonton, New Jersey, where we had moved so my mother could work on her doctoral thesis." The future anthropologist's mother was working on articles for various encyclopedias at the time of her daughter's birth. While she subsequently devoted most of her time to her family and left it to her daughter to realize many unfulfilled ambitions, she struggled unceasingly to maintain her own intellectual life and to pass these values on to her children.

Sometimes it is not specifically the mother's activities, but an overall expectation about female members of the family which has been influential in shaping the direction of a woman's life. For example:

My grandmothers and great-grandmothers ran plantations while the men were off fighting wars or sitting in legislatures; they were in charge of the grist mill or the general store while the men ran the farm or ranch; they were the local animal doctors before there were veterinarians; one was a botanist and specialist of

some repute in medicinal herbs. . . . I don't believe it
has ever occurred to anyone on either side of the family
that a woman could be or ought to be "a mere housewife"; and hardly a man in the family would be likely
to choose a wife who saw herself in that single role.[5]

Millicent McIntosh, formerly the president of Barnard
College, describes her mother, a minister in the Friends
Meeting, a graduate of Bryn Mawr in its first class, and a
hard worker for such unpopular causes as women's suffrage, peace, and racial equality, as "the earliest and most
profound influence on my life."[6] But she also came
under the influence of another family model, her mother's oldest sister, M. Carey Thomas, the founder and
president of Bryn Mawr and a strong-minded feminist.
Few Bryn Mawr students during the time of M. Carey
Thomas failed to be affected by her belief that it was the
responsibility of educated women not to be submerged by
parenthood or marriage.

As a parent, then, you must make very certain that
your daughter knows feminine role models who are successful in masculine-dominated fields. If you do not have
a career yourself, and have no serious investment in past
or future work experience, it will be much more difficult
for your daughter to integrate the concept of work and
achievement into her idea of femininity. What more can I
say? I do not necessarily believe that every woman can or
should, in midlife, return to or begin a career. To do so
poses many difficulties to which I cannot address myself
here, but of which I am well aware and about which I
have written in the past[7] (and will write more in the
future).

But I suspect that many of you who will be reading
this book are young enough and energetic enough to
begin a career now, even if you did not plan for one
originally. If you are wondering about the effect of this
on your daughter, I can only say that I think it will be
beneficial in terms of the additional avenues which will

appear open to her by virtue of the example you set.

If this is not possible for you, it will be even more important to make sure that your daughter gets to know other achieving women. Does she know *any*? In the past, teachers were often the only career-oriented women known to children of either sex. Achieving women in most other fields are to be found these days in most communities, but they are not always highly visible. Perhaps you could change to a woman doctor or dentist. It is more difficult to introduce your child to a woman lawyer, engineer, college professor, architect, or scientist, unless such a woman happens to be among your personal circle of friends. If this is the case, or if you know other women with careers, especially if they are married and are working in masculine fields, I urge you to invite them to your home when your daughter will be there and try to promote an active friendship. If there are any such women in your neighborhood, perhaps you can become acquainted with them if you make a special effort to do so. Take your children to community activities and neighborhood get-togethers where women of varied lifestyles will be present. A Fourth of July parade may be just the right occasion to point out to your daughter that the mayor of your town, marching with your local congresswoman, is a Ms.

8

History Lessons

Having your daughter learn from observation that you and other women you know consider meaningful work a significant and satisfying part of life is one of the most important things you can do to create the same expectation in her for her own future.

She can also learn from the past.

It is remarkable that before the current women's movement made many of us conscious of the shortcomings and oversights of our educational processes, so little attention was given to the history of women. Before the 1960s women's studies courses—including women's history—did not even exist. Today they are proliferating at the college level, but they reach only the relatively small proportion of students who are already interested enough in the topic to elect the course. Few, if any, high school or junior high school students—not to mention those in elementary school—are ever exposed to any

course which covers this topic in even a fragmentary
fashion. Eventually, changes will occur—if we, as
women, fight for them.

But, in the meantime, I think you will have to tutor
your daughter in the history of women. I don't mean for-
mally, of course, but there are many things you can do
informally to introduce her to the achieving women of
the past as well as those currently in the news.

If you yourself are relatively unfamiliar with the history of women, I suggest that you do some preliminary
reading to acquaint yourself with the topic in a general
way. There is such a variety of books on women available today, many of them in paperback, that it is difficult to know where to begin. However, Elizabeth Janeway's *Man's World, Woman's Place* is one good starting
point which serves to put the present plight of women
into historical perspective. *Woman in Sexist Society*,
edited by Vivian Gornick and Barbara K. Moran, contains many eye-opening, thought-provoking essays. And
Virginia Woolf's *A Room of One's Own*, published in
1929, is the best answer I've found to that old recurring
question, "Why haven't women ever accomplished anything in art?" or music or writing or what have you. I
think every thoughtful woman should read this short
book over and over again.

Eleanor Flexner's book, *Century of Struggle: The
Woman's Rights Movement in the United States*, is a
good factual account of the suffrage movement.
Morningstar, a Biography of Lucy Stone, by Eleanor
Hayes, is one of the more interesting biographies of individual women's rights leaders. *The Feminine Mystique*,
by Betty Friedan, published in 1963, is the book which
started the current women's movement, and is well worth
reading if you haven't already.

Personally, I think that these books are all worthwhile
additions to your permanent library, not only for your

own reference but to be available for your daughter when she is old enough to read them. An intelligent eighth grader is capable of reading just about anything, and by this age writing assignments are often given at school. My own experience has been that as a parent I am often asked for suggestions of topics to write about—and I suspect that you will be too. This is one way to make up for (in a small way) the appalling deficiencies of the average school's social studies program. Two of my own daughters have already written term papers on topics relating to women's rights, one on the suffrage movement and the other on women in the labor force. Among the books which have recently been selected for school book reports at my house are Margaret Mead's autobiography, *Blackberry Winter*, and Virginia Woolf's *A Room of One's Own*.

Of course, it isn't necessary to wait until your daughter reaches adolescence to start her reading about women. Biographies written especially for younger readers provide the ideal introduction, and I would make a point of seeking out those which are appropriate to your daughter's age level. Almost every child reads about Madame Curie, Clara Barton, and Helen Keller, but what about Elizabeth Blackwell (*Challenge to Become a Doctor*, Leah Lurie Heyne, Feminist Press), *Shirley Chisholm* (Susan Brownmiller, Doubleday), *Lucretia Mott* (Dorothy Sterling, Doubleday) and Margaret Chase Smith (*The Senator From Maine*, Alice Fleming, Crowell)? There are many other good biographies written especially for young readers, and others are still to be written. Your public library will be the best place to find them.

Good collections of biographical works include *Women of Courage* (Dorothy Nathan, Random House) and *Growing Up Female in America* (edited by Eve Merriam, Doubleday). There is also a major biograph-

ical work which I think should be on the shelf of every
home including a daughter: the three-volume *Notable
American Women*, prepared under the auspices of Radcliffe College and published in 1971 by the Harvard University Press ($25 in paperback). This is an invaluable
reference work, contains the material needed for in-
numerable school reports as well as bibliographies for
each subject, and is highly readable. Having acquired the
work shortly after its publication, I now wonder how I
ever managed without it.

But the exploration of women's place in history need
not be limited to books. More and more worthwhile programs on topics of concern to women are currently
appearing on TV and I recently read that a new series on
famous women is in preparation. Movies are another
possibility, but mainly for the future—unfortunately the
first movie directed specifically to issues related to
women's liberation (*The Stepford Wives*) was a gro-
tesque and dismal failure. Classic dramas, like Ibsen's *A
Doll's House*, more effectively state the conflicts of
women in traditional roles.

If you are alert to what is going on in your community, you will at least occasionally find opportunities
to take your daughter to dramatic productions concerned with women of achievement or issues of interest to
women. From time to time there may be art exhibits of
works by women artists or photographers. To keep
abreast of these events, it is obviously necessary to follow
the local newspaper.

Another opportunity I wouldn't pass up to make history come alive is the chance to visit the birthplaces or
homes of women of distinction. Some of these sites are
historic landmarks, and I think it is worthwhile to go out
of your way to see them. I have found that my own
daughters were particularly interested in the birthplace
of Maria Mitchell on Nantucket, which we visited more

than once while vacationing there, and the home of Harriet Beecher Stowe in Hartford, adjoining Mark Twain's. I had not realized before going through the Stowe home that the author of *Uncle Tom's Cabin* produced a book a year for more than twenty years (her writing was the family's chief source of income), painted in both oil and watercolor (many of her works hang in the house and show considerable talent), and also wrote hymns. She accomplished all of this while raising seven children. My visit to her home in Hartford made a lasting impression on me and the two daughters who were with me, and I wondered why I hadn't taken them sooner.

Because I think visits to historic houses are such an effective way of learning history enjoyably, I am including a list of historic houses in the United States which pertain to women of achievement. I hope you will take your daughter to visit as many of these historic places as possible.

ALABAMA

TUSCALOOSA

Friedman Home, 1010 Greensboro Avenue. This house was once the home of Virginia Tunstall Clay-Clopton (1825-1915), Alabama suffragist and antebellum society leader. Mrs. Clay-Clopton served as president of the Alabama Equal Rights Association from 1896 until 1900. Her endorsement of woman suffrage added greatly to its prestige in this period of strong resistance. At the age of seventy-five, she published a volume of memoirs entitiled *A Belle of the Fifties*. Open Sun. 2-5 and by appointment.

TUSCUMBIA

Ivy Green, Birthplace of Helen Keller, 300 W. North Common. Helen Keller (1880-1968), author and social worker, is best known for her willpower, courage, and outstanding achievements in spite of her blindness and deafness. Her brave outlook on life has been an inspiration for thousands of people. "I seldom think about my limitations, and they never make me sad. Perhaps there is just a touch of yearning at times, but it is vague, like a breeze among flowers. The wind passes, and the flowers are content." This house is the scene of the annual summer theater presentation of *The Miracle Worker*, based on Helen Keller's childhood and her remarkable teacher, Anne Sullivan. Open Mon.—Sat. 8:30-4:30, Sun. 1-4:30; closed Christmas and New Year's Day.

ARKANSAS

EUREKA SPRINGS

Hatchet Hall, Carry Nation's last home, 35 Steel Street. A zealous temperance reformer, Carry Nation (1846-1911) spent the last three years of her life operating this boarding house. In 1892, she helped found a county chapter of the W.C.T.U. Through colorful tactics, she publicized the prohibition cause more widely than any previous person. Open daily 9:30-5; closed Sun. during summer.

CALIFORNIA

SAN DIEGO

Casa de Lopez (The Candle Shop), *3890 Twiggs Street.* Helen Hunt Jackson (1830-1885), author and crusader for Indian rights, modeled Father Antonio Ubach, the character in her novel *Ramona* after the man who lived in this home. Mrs. Jackson was highly acclaimed as a poet and novelist, and *Ramona* was her finest achievement. Three movies have been made of the novel, and in southern California, it inspires an annual pageant at Hemet. Open during business hours.

CONNECTICUT

HARTFORD

Harriet Beecher Stowe House, 73 Forest Street. This

house was occupied by Harriet Beecher Stowe (1811-1896), author of *Uncle Tom's Cabin*, and her husband from 1873 until 1896. *Uncle Tom's Cabin* was the pinnacle in Mrs. Stowe's long literary career. Her creative impulse sprang from a strong reaction against slavery. The novel depicts the passionate pain and sorrow of maternal loss, which she experienced in her own life as a mother. Open Tues.-Sat. 9:30-4, Sun. 1-4; closed holidays.

FLORIDA

CROSS CREEK

Marjorie Kinnan Rawlings House, State Road 325. This was the home of Marjorie Kinnan Rawlings, novelist, and the setting of *The Yearling*, her Pulitzer Prize winning novel of a boy's love for his pet fawn. Open daily 9-5.

GEORGIA

SAVANNAH

Andrew Low House, 329 Abercorn Street, home of Juliette Gordon Low (1860-1927). On March 12, 1912, Juliette Gordon Low formed the first Girl Guide units in America (the feminine counterpart of the Boy Scouts), and in 1915, the Girl Scouts of America was organized with Juliette Low as president. Even while suffering from cancer, she devoted her last few years to the organization she founded. Open Mon.-Sat. 10:30-4:30; closed holidays.

Wayne-Gordon House, 10 Oglethorpe Ave. E., birthplace of Juliette Gordon Low. Juliette Low, founder of the Girl Scouts of America, was born in this house to William Washington Gordon II and Eleanor Lytle Gordon. She is said to have inherited her wit, charm, and artistic talent from her energetic and dominating mother, but relied heavily upon her father's judgment and affection. Open Mon.-Sat. 9-4:30, Sun. 2-4:30; closed Thanksgiving, Christmas, and New Year's Day.

ILLINOIS

CHICAGO

Hull House, 800 S. Halsted Street, on Chicago Circle Campus. Jane Addams (1860-1935), settlement founder, social reformer, and peace worker had a visionary plan to connect privileged young people, especially young women like herself, with the real world. In 1889, she converted Hull House, located in the heart of a crowded ethnic neighborhood, into a settlement house, which became the center of social reform activities. Her outstanding book, *Twenty Years at Hull House*, ranks among the great American autobiographies. From 1911 to 1914, she served as first vice-president of the National American Woman Suffrage Association. She was the first American woman to win the Nobel prize for peace, and she gave her prize money, some $16,000 to the Women's International League. Open Mon.-Fri. 10-4.

Rest Cottage, Frances Willard House, 1730 Chicago Ave. Frances E. Willard (1839-1898), temperance leader and woman's suffrage advocate, was elected president of the national W.C.T.U. in 1879. She felt the W.C.T.U. could give women an opportunity to take a more active role in society beyond the family circle. She was responsible for awakening the interest of thousands of women in political affairs. Open Mon.-Fri. 9-12, 1:30-4:30, Sat., Sun., and holidays by appointment.

INDIANA

GENEVA

Limberlost Cabin, Sixth and Williams Streets. Gene Stratton Porter (1863-1924), author and photographer, designed this two-story "cabin." During her lifetime, Mrs. Porter's novels enjoyed a phenomenal popularity, second only to those of Scott and Dickens. Her most popular works were *A Girl of the Limberlost* and *Freckles*, which praised .lives in harmony with nature. Open daily 9-12, 1-5, Sun. 1-5; closed Mon. during winter.

Rome City

Gene Stratton Porter Home, Indiana Route 9. This was the second "cabin" designed by Mrs. Porter. Open Summer daily 8:30-5:30, winter Tues.-Sat. 9-12, 1-5.

Kansas

Argonia

Salter House. This was the home of Susanna Medora Salter, elected mayor of Argonia, Kansas, on April 4, 1887, the first woman in the United States to hold such a position. She served for one year and was paid one dollar for her services.

Medicine Lodge

Carry Nation Home, 211 W. Fowler Avenue. This was the home of Carry Nation at the peak of her temperance "hatchetation" raids. She would enter saloons, hatchet in hand, and smash liquor bottles, lewd paintings, and furniture. Open evenings 6-10.

Louisiana

Cloutierville

Bayou Folk Museum, Louisiana Route 1. This was the home of Kate Chopin (1851-1904), the popular author who wrote about women's conflicts involving love, marriage, and art. In 1899 she published her novel *The Awakening*, an extraordinary and in many ways her best piece of writing. Open March-Nov., Sat. and Sun. 2-6 and by appointment.

Maine

Brunswick

Harriet Beecher Stowe House, 63 Federal Street. It was in this house that Mrs. Stowe (1811-1896) wrote her famous antislavery novel, *Uncle Tom's Cabin.* Open daily.

Ellsworth

Stanwood Homestead, Route 3. This was the home of

Cordelia Stanwood, a pioneer ornithologist, nature photographer, and author. Open June 15-Labor Day, 10-4, and by appointment.

FARMINGTON

Nordica Homestead. Lillian Norton Nordica (1857-1914), an opera singer known as the "Lily of the North," was a leading member of the Metropolitan Opera Company from 1893 to 1907. Her forte was as a Wagnerian soprano. Away from the stage, she was an ardent suffragist. Open June-Labor Day, Tues.-Sun. 10-12, 1-5, May, Sept., and Oct. by appointment.

POLAND SPRING VICINITY

Shaker Village. This is one of the last remaining Shaker communities in the country established by Mother Ann Lee (1736-1784), founder of the United Society of Believers in Christ's Second Appearing. She advocated equal rights and responsibilities for women in the Shaker society, thus anticipating the feminist movement in America. The first Shaker village was established near Albany, New York, in 1776. Open summer for tours.

SOUTH BERWICK

Hamilton House, Vaughan's Lane. Sarah Orne Jewett (1849-1909) used this mansion as the setting for her novel, *The Tory Lover.* The literature of this talented author held the quality of reality. She is best known for *The Country of the Pointed Firs*, one of the unquestionable classics of American prose writing. Open June-Sept. Tues., Thurs., Fri., Sun. 1-5.

MARYLAND

BALTIMORE

Mother Seton House, 600 N. Paca Street. Mother Seton (1774-1821), founder and head of the first American sisterhood, conducted a Roman Catholic girls' school in this house in 1808. Elizabeth Seton was converted to Catholicism after the death of her husband. Open Sat. and Sun. 1-4, except holidays.

GLEN ECHO

Clara Barton House, 5801 Oxford Road. Clara Barton (1821-1912) was founder and for twenty-three years president of the American Red Cross. To the thousands of Civil War soldiers she helped treat, she was known as the "Angel of the Battlefield." This home served as Red Cross headquarters during the later years of her presidency. She was a feminist by lifelong conviction and made clear her support of suffrage and equal pay for equal work. Open Tues.-Sat. 1-5; closed holidays.

MASSACHUSETTS

AMESBURY

Mary Baker Eddy Historic House, 227 Main Street. Mary Baker Eddy (1821-1910), founder of the Church of Christ, Scientist wrote her early teaching manuscripts, including *The Science of Man*, while living here. Upon meeting the faith healer, Phineas Parkhurst Quimby, an important change occurred in Mrs. Eddy's life. Many of Quimby's views, including those which held the cause and cure of disease to be mental, became her own. She dramatized a startling new approach to religion. Open May-Oct. Tues.-Sun. 1-4; closed holidays.

CONCORD

Orchard House, 399 Lexington Road, Route 2A. Louisa May Alcott (1832-1888), author, wrote the first part of her novel *Little Women* while living in this house. *Little Women*, based on the childhood of Louisa, brought instant fame to the author and created an incessant demand for her books. She was the first woman to register in Concord when Massachusetts gave women the vote in 1879. Open Mid April-early Nov., Mon.-Sat. 10-4:30, Sun. 1-4:30.

HANCOCK

Hancock Shaker Village. This is the third oldest of the Shaker communities built in the late eighteenth cen-

tury following the founding of the first Shaker Village
by Mothen Ann Lee in 1776. Open June-Oct. 15, daily
9:30-5.

LYNN

Mary Baker Eddy Residence, 12 Broad Street. One of
the residences of Mary Baker Eddy, founder of the
Church of Christ, Scientist. Open May-Oct., Wed.-Sat.
11:30-4, Sun. 2-5, Nov.-Apr. by appointment.

NANTUCKET

Maria Mitchell Birthplace, 1 Vestal Street. Built in
1790, this house was the birthplace of Maria Mitchell,
the Vassar teacher who discovered a comet in 1847. As
a young girl, she would assist her father in checking
chronometers for the Nantucket whaling fleet by
stellar observation. She became one of the great
teachers at Vassar, encouraged many students to enter
the field of astronomy, and worked for the recognition
of women in the sciences. Open June 15-Sept. 15,
Mon.-Fri. 10-12, 2-5, Sat. 10-12.

NORTH OXFORD

Clara Barton Birthplace, Clara Barton Road. Clara
Barton, founder of the American Red Cross, was born
in this early nineteenth century house. Open July-
Aug., Sun., Tues., Wed., Fri., Sat. 1-5, and throughout
year by appointment.

STOUGHTON

Mary Baker Eddy Historical House, 133 Central Street.
The founder of Christian Science lived here off and on
from 1868 to 1879. Open May-Oct. Tues.-Sun. 1-4;
closed holidays.

SWAMPSCOTT

Mary Baker Eddy Historic House, 23 Paradise Road.
Mrs. Eddy rented an apartment in this house in 1866
and experienced a spiritual healing through reading
the Bible. Open May 15-Oct. 31, Mon.-Sat. 10-5, Sun.
2-5, Nov. 1-May 14, Tues.-Sun. 1-4; closed holidays.

MISSISSIPPI

HOLLY SPRINGS

Walter Place, 331 Chulahoma Ave. Birthplace of Dr. Anne Walter Fearn, who spent over thirty years in China as a surgeon and philanthropic worker. Dr. Fearn went to China in 1893 after receiving her M.D. from Woman's Medical College. Open by appointment only.

NEBRASKA

RED CLOUD

Willa Cather Childhood Home, Third and Cedar Street. Willa Sibert Cather (1873-1947), author, learned about life on the frontier while living in this home. She moved here with her family at the age of ten, leaving the stability of the Virginia farming life for the frontier and spaces greater than she had ever known. In her simple and elegiac novels, Willa Cather records the drive of strong-willed persons to achievement and their discovery of how illusory success can be. Her novels emphasize feeling rather than thought and the act of doing rather than reflection. *My Antonia* was the finest of her prairie novels, and in 1922 she won the Pulitzer Prize for *One of Ours.* Open Apr. 1-Nov. 15, Mon.-Sat. 8-5, Sun. 1-5, Nov. 16-Apr. 1, Mon.-Fri. 8-5.

NEW HAMPSHIRE

NORTH GROTON

Mary Baker Eddy Historical House. The founder of the Church of Christ, Scientist lived here from 1855 until 1860 with her second husband, Dr. Daniel Paterson. Open May 30-Oct., Sun. 2-5 and by appointment.

NEW YORK

AUBURN

Harriet Tubman House, 180 South Street. Harriet Tubman (1820?-1913), fugitive slave and rescuer of

slaves, Civil War scout and nurse, escaped from slavery
in 1849 and helped to free some three hundred Negroes
from their bondage. She was a deeply religious person
who never doubted that her actions were guided by
divine commands. Harriet Tubman established the
Harriet Tubman Home for Indigent Aged Negroes in
this house. Illiterate herself, she promoted the estab-
lishment of freedmen's schools in the South. Through
the years, she attended many suffrage meetings. She
was known as "the Moses of her people." Open by
appointment.

ROCHESTER

Susan B. Anthony House, 17 Madison Street. Susan B.
Anthony was the woman suffrage leader who was
more responsible than any other individual for the
adoption of the Nineteenth Amendment. In 1850, she
met Elizabeth Cady Stanton, who proposed, at the first
woman's rights convention, a resolution demanding
woman suffrage. From that day to the end of her life,
Susan Anthony devoted her energies to securing the
vote for women. From 1892 until 1900 she served as
president of the National American Woman Suffrage
Association. Open Wed.-Sat. 11-4 and by appointment.

VERMONT

MIDDLEBURY

Emma Willard House, Middlebury College Campus.
Emma Willard (1787-1870) was the sixteenth daughter
of a political liberal who encouraged her in intellectual pursuits. By the time she was fourteen, her father
was calling her from domestic duties with her mother
to listen to an essay he had written or to engage in
philosophical discussions. In 1814 she opened the
Middlebury Female Seminary in her home, making
available to women the classical and scientific subjects previously available only in colleges for men. In
1821 she established the Troy Female Seminary, which
turned out two hundred teachers before the first normal school was founded in the United States. In 1895

the school was renamed the Emma Willard School. Open as the admissions office of Middlebury College.

VIRGINIA

RICHMOND

Ellen Glasgow House, 1 West Main Street. Ellen Glasgow (1873-1945) was a member of Virginia society and a novelist, whose works indicate that she was a feminist. Though her direct participation in the movement was governed more by her sister's interest in it than by her own, she was, nevertheless, active in the Equal Suffrage League of Virginia, organized at the Glasgow home in 1909. Though considered a minor literary figure, Ellen Glasgow's novels record that peculiar American conflict between professed idealism and pragmatic achievement. Open Mon.-Fri. 8:30-4:30.

WEST VIRGINIA

HILLSBORO

Stulting House, Pearl S. Buck Birthplace, U.S. Route 219. This house was built by the greatgrandfather of novelist Pearl S. Buck (1892—1973), who grew up in Chinkiang China, on the Yangtse River. After the publication of her novel *The Good Earth,* one of the most popular novels of the twentieth century, she received the Pulitzer Prize and in 1938 she was awarded the Nobel Prize for Literature. In 1941 she founded The East and West Association to establish better relations between Asia and the United States, and in 1951 she was elected to the American Academy of Arts and Letters, one of only two women in that body of fifty life members. Open Mon.-Sat. 9-5, Sun. 1-5; closed Thanksgiving, Christmas, and New Year's Day.

9

Fathers and Daughters

It is not only a girl's mother and other female models of past and present who are influential in shaping her concept of what her future life will be like. Her father also plays a crucial role in this process.

Obviously, if a woman is career-oriented her husband is more likely to be sympathetic to the idea of his wife's working. This is particularly true if his wife is working in a demanding career. Most women just can't succeed in high level professional work *without* their husband's support and cooperation. The lack of it is too undermining. Most women who are successful, and are also married, specifically mention their husband's help and support as major factors in their success.

A child of either sex growing up in such an atmosphere is going to assimilate the idea that it is alright for mother to work and that dad approves and does his share to keep the household running smoothly. Parents like these are setting the stage for a child to reach adulthood without a set of built in sex-role-stereotypes.

This is one situation in which the father's role is very important. He is reinforcing his wife's position as an independent adult with a right to her own career. By his choice of her as his wife, he not only shows that he approves this lifestyle for women—but that he prefers it.

There is another kind of family in which the father's attitude and behavior toward the daughter may be even *more* significant. I am speaking of the family in which the wife is not career-oriented but is, instead, a housewife with traditional values. In this situation it is more or less up to the father to give his daughter the idea that girls can do anything they choose to do. There are exceptions to every rule, but in general I think that every middle-class girl who achieves success must have had either an achieving mother as a model, or a father who offered particular encouragement. Ideally both conditions are present—but they are not always necessary.

I singled out the middle class in the last paragraph because in lower socioeconomic classes the situation is somewhat different. If a woman is working it is more often a matter of necessity than choice. Whether the mother is working or not, the hardships of life in general and of women's lives in particular are likely to shape a girl's attitudes and expectations in a different way. Often education and career are seen by a bright girl as the only way out of a bad situation. These goals are not necessarily integrated into the expectation of marriage and family as they are more likely to be in a middle-class family.

In a study of able college women at Stanford University during the early sixties, those classified as "autonomous developers" most often had dynamic fathers with supporting wives. They reported close identifications with both parents but had unusually warm relationships with their fathers.[1] In another study comparing honors graduates of a midwestern university, the married professionals reported having been much closer to their fathers than either single professionals or homemakers. The married professionals were likely to describe themselves as particularly like their father intellectually, while the homemakers tended to describe themselves as resembling their mother or both parents. In addition, this group was far more likely to recall their mothers and fathers as very close to each other. The married professionals viewed their fathers as more intellectual than either of the other two groups, while the homemakers' fathers—not surprisingly—tended to be more traditionally oriented.[2]

A study of twenty-five successful women executives also found that these women reported that their relationships with both parents during early childhood were extremely close and warm. Relationships with fathers were recalled as atypical—warmer, closer, more supportive, and more sharing. These daughters had shared many personal interests and enthusiasms with their fathers. Both parents had high aspirations for their daughters. The mothers in almost all cases represented typical feminine role models, but they supported their daughters' complete freedom to explore male roles. The fathers encouraged their daughter's femininity but participated with them in male activities, encouraged them to compete and to internalize their own standards of achievement.[3]

In other words, these women who have experienced outstanding success in a man's world were definitely treated by their families as people who were female yet had open to them all of the behaviors and activities open to either sex. They were able to internalize achievement striving in a warm, supportive environment before they reached the age where they would be exposed to the inevitable conflicts about achievement goals for women.

The effect of a nontraditional father with high expectations for women can be clearly seen on children of both sexes in the family of Samuel Blackwell, a prosperous English sugar refiner who was an active Dissenter and lay preacher in the Independent Church. Blackwell was a deeply religious man who championed social reform, women's rights, temperance, and the abolition of slavery. (His wife was reportedly beautiful and spirited and played a traditional supporting role.) The Blackwells had twelve children, nine of whom survived infancy. Because Dissenters' children were barred from schools, Samuel Blackwell engaged private tutors who taught the girls the same subjects as the boys—an unheard-of procedure in the early nineteenth century. In 1832 the family moved to America, where they continued their abolitionist activities while living first in New York, then in New Jersey, and finally in Cleveland.

The later accomplishments of Samuel Blackwell's children were remarkable for any era but particularly for a time when most women found few avenues open to them. One daughter became a newspaper correspondent, another an author and artist. Elizabeth Blackwell, born in 1821, was the first woman of modern times to graduate in medicine. After being refused admission by every medical school in Philadelphia and New York as well as by Harvard and Yale, she received her medical degree from Geneva College in West Central New York in 1849. Though she encountered frustration, disappointment, and discrimination throughout her life, she had a distinguished career as a reformer and physician, founding a medical college for women in New York. Emily Blackwell, her younger sister, also became a physician, receiving her medical degree from Western Reserve University in Cleveland in 1854 and later joining her sister in New York.

Not only did the Blackwell women achieve, but Blackwell men married achieving women! Samuel Charles married Antoinette Louisa Brown, an author, lecturer, feminist leader, and the first woman ordained as a minister in America. He supported his wife's feminist principles in the same way that his younger brother, Henry, supported the feminist principles and activities of his equally famous wife, Lucy Stone. An Oberlin graduate and classmate of Antoinette Brown, Lucy traveled and lectured widely on women's rights and abolition. She established a precedent in 1855 which had few followers until more than a century later. With her husband's support, she kept her own name when she married, and at the ceremony they read a protest against traditional marriage laws.

Recently, while rereading the history of the Blackwell family and considering the influence of Samuel Blackwell upon his children, I was struck not only with his insistence on the equal education of boys and girls but the influence of his liberal thought and his own involvement with social reform.

Another father-influenced family with a strong religious orientation, in which several children achieved lasting fame, was that of Lyman Beecher, an eminent Congregational minister. Beecher fathered thirteen children, of which Harriet Beecher Stowe was the seventh child and fourth daughter. Harriet's own mother died when she was four, and not liking the stepmother who joined the family two years later, she turned to her father for guidance and to her younger brother, Henry Ward, for companionship and play. Two of Harriet's sisters also achieved prominence in their day, Catharine Esther

Beecher as an educator and Isabella Beecher Hooker as a suffrage leader.

Was there a special significance in the religious orientation of these two fathers who produced such successful and unusual daughters?

I do not know, but in reviewing biographical data on the twenty women starred (a sign of distinction) in *American Men of Science* before 1920, I found that three of twenty had fathers who were ministers, while the father of a fourth was a college professor who had first considered the ministry and remained deeply religious throughout his life.

Two other occupations which seemed disproportionately represented among this group were those of farmer (four) and merchant (four). Do these three occupations—minister, farmer, merchant—have something in common? What occurs to me is that they are all occupations in which a father is either at home a good deal of the time, or in which he might easily take a child of either sex along to work with him.

One of the difficulties with today's nuclear family, especially in metropolitan areas, is that the father is at home for such short periods of time that it is difficult for him to make his influence felt. This is of particular importance when the mother is a housewife, for there tends to be little exposure to the values of the working world, or the values of any world beyond the home, for the children in such a family.

10

Having a Small Family

Elizabeth Blackwell, America's first woman doctor, was the third daughter and third child in a family of twelve children.

Antoinette Brown Blackwell, the first woman to be ordained as a minister, was the fourth daughter and seventh child in a family of ten children.

Harriet Beecher Stowe was the seventh child and fourth daughter in a family of thirteen children.

These outstandingly successful women are exceptional not only for their accomplishments but also to some extent for their position in the family. All studies which have related eminence to birth order and position in the family have found that individuals of outstanding intellectual accomplishment, especially in science, are likely to be either first born or only children.

Altus[1] has summarized the relevant studies on eminence and birth order. Sir Francis Galton's *English Men of*

Science, published in 1874, was the first investigation to bring this relationship to light. Galton collected biographical data on scientists who met objective criteria such as being a Fellow of the Royal Society, and found more only sons and first-born sons than could have been accounted for by chance.

A generation later, Havelock Ellis published *A Study of British Genius*. Ellis selected the 975 eminent men and 55 eminent women from the 66 volumes of the *Dictionary of National Biography*, choosing those to whom three or more pages were devoted but excluding those who were of the nobility or whom he judged to be notorious rather than famous. Like Galton, Ellis found a higher proportion of first-born than intermediate children. He also found that the youngest was favored over the intermediate children, though not to the same extent.

About the same time that the Ellis study appeared in England, the American psychologist Cattell published data based on 855 American scientists. Cattell's findings paralleled those of Ellis, with oldest children and then the youngest occurring most frequently among the eminent.

In 1915, a study of Italian university professors found that twice as many were first-born as could have been expected by chance. The data did not allow conclusions to be drawn about the prevalence of youngest children in the sample. However, in a study of American men of letters, both youngest and eldest children appeared in greater than expected numbers.

First-borns and last-borns are overrepresented among Rhodes Scholars. And of those listed in *Who's Who*, 64 percent of the representatives of two-child families are first born, as are 50 percent of those from three-child families. If these were chance distributions, the figures should be 50 percent and 33 percent.

While there have been few studies of eminent women, the available evidence suggests that exactly the same relationships hold true. Among twenty women starred for distinctive accomplishment among those listed in *American Men of Science* prior to 1920, six were only children and six others were eldest children, while five were youngest children. Only a quarter of these successful women were middle children.

In the study of twenty-five successful women executives to which I have referred earlier, all were first born and female. All were either only children or the eldest in an all-girl family of no more than three female siblings.[2]

Among the twelve professional women in the sciences and other male-dominated fields selected to participate in a conference on women and success, half were first-born. In 58.3 percent of the families, there were only two children.[3]

The reasons for these findings are not clear. Only children and firstborns are overrepresented in graduate school, and one line of thought is that their superior education accounts for greater intellectual accomplishment in later years. However, this would seem unlikely in such fields as art and literature. On the other hand, the differences between first-borns and other children—including their greater educational accomplishments—may be due to greater motivation or higher intelligence.

First-borns do tend to make better grades in school, and most studies also find first-borns to have higher IQs. Among the very bright, first-borns are found in disproportionate numbers. In Terman's famous study of gifted children (those with IQs over 140), eldest children occurred most frequently, followed by youngest children. Eldest children have been noted to constitute 61 percent of the student population at Yale and 66 percent at Reed College, both of which have very rigorous admissions standards.[4] According to a 1964 survey, 60 percent of the National Merit Finalists who come from families of two, three, four, and five children were first-born. The National Merit Finalists data showed a stairstep progression downward with each successive birth position.[5]

A similar hierarchy was noted in a study of IQs in a total population of almost 400,000 nineteen-year-old men born in the Netherlands from 1944 through 1947.[6] They were tested as part of an examination to determine their fitness for military service.

In all social classes and family sizes, first-borns made a better showing than did later borns. In two-, three-, and four-child families, there was a decline in intellectual performance with each birth position. First-borns did best, followed by second-borns, then by third-borns and fourth-borns.

Family size also had a significant effect on intelligence, with those from two-child families doing best. There was a decrement in IQs with each increase in family size, although this was less true in the highest social class. Contrary to expectations, only children did less well than those from two-child families. Because it covered such a large number of subjects in a total population, and controlled for social class (which many other studies have not done), the Dutch study is of particular significance.

How can these findings, as well as earlier studies relating intelligence and eminence to birth position, be explained?

Galton felt that first-borns' greater eminence was due to the law of primogeniture, which meant that the eldest son was likely to inherit and thus to have the means to follow his tastes and educational inclinations. Galton also thought that only children and first-borns were given more companionship and more responsibility.

Recently, psychologists have noted that first-borns

show greater conscience development than later children, are more dependent, and have a greater need for approval. However, these findings are not entirely consistent.[7] Some investigators have found that parents tend to be stricter with first-borns and more permissive with later children. Fathers are more likely to participate in the disciplining of the first-born. It seems possible that first-born and only children are often the recipients of higher expectations of achievement, which may cause them to work harder in school, show more intellectual curiosity in and out of school, and increase their intellectual stature as a result.

There is absolutely no reason to suppose that there could be a genetic reason for the apparent intellectual superiority of first-borns. All genetic models assume that genes are randomly distributed without regard to birth order. However, it is obvious that the environment for the first of two children will be considerably different from that of the fifth of nine. And, within the same family, the position of the first is very different from that of the last.

Recently a University of Michigan professor, Robert Zajonc, came up with an ingenious explanation for the decreasing IQs found in large families. Since a newborn infant has very little to bring with her in the way of intellectual accomplishment, her arrival in the family lowers the intellectual average considerably. The same thing happens with each successive child so that the amount of stimulation available to the youngest child, in terms of adult intellectual standards, is the least of all. Of course, Zajonc says, if the intervals between children are very large, the negative effects of birth order can even be reversed. That is, if a second child is born when the first has attained 80 percent of his adult intellectual growth, she will be entering a more favorable intellectual atmosphere than the first.[8]

In support of his theory, Zajonc points to studies which show that, in contrast to an average IQ of 100 in children born singly, twins average 95.7 and triplets 91.6.

However, as he admits, there's one problem. Why didn't only children do best of all? According to the Dutch data, the intellectual level of the only child was equivalent to that of the eldest child in a four-child family. (The highest scores were obtained by the eldest in a two-child family and then the eldest in a three-child family and then the eldest in a four-child family.)

Zajonc, an only child himself who managed to acquire a Ph.D. anyway, attributes this finding to the fact that the only child has nobody to teach. The Dutch data showed a sharper drop in intellectual levels between the last two children in all size families than that shown between successive children in other birth positions. While the IQs of later born children in large families (five children and up) begin to rise, there is a drop for the last child in every family size.

This suggests that there is a handicap to being the baby and the spoiled darling of the family. It is not clear at all why the data on intellectual performance of youngest children is largely contrary to the data on eminence, which places youngest children in the most favored position after eldest and only children. Perhaps youngest children receive some special benefits of parental attention which result in stronger motivation for later accomplishment.

Zajonc's explanation is only a theory, but it does appear to fit the facts reasonably well.

And the facts suggest that in terms of family planning, if you want your daughter to achieve you should have her first in a family of two children. Of course, there's no reason why they can't both be achievers. But if Zajonc's theory is correct, you should arrange for your second to tutor a neighbor's child.

Of course, it is essential to remember that the statistics presented in this chapter are averages only. The stairwise progressions in intelligence among successive children do not occur in every family, and highly successful people—both men and women—have been born in all family positions. Averages do not allow* individual predictions. But, if you are playing the odds, the eldest in a two-child family would have to be picked for the winner.

It's a bit curious to reflect that the ideal three-or-four-child family of a few years ago, desired so widely by well-educated parents, actually did not provide the optimum environment for the intellectual growth of the children. At the same time, having several children places severe limitations on the career aspirations and commitments of the mother.

For the mother who does have serious career interests, a one-or-two child family has definite advantages over a large brood. According to the Census Bureau Population Division, there is growing acceptance of the small family. In 1967, 6.1 percent of women aged eighteen to twenty-four said they expected to have only one child in their lifetime. By 1973, 9.6 percent expected to have only one child—an increase of more than 58 percent.

With increasing concern over population growth and the inflationary cost of living and education, it seems likely that the number of couples who choose to have only one or two children will continue to increase. And as far as the intellectual growth of the children is concerned, this will be all to the good.

II

Encouraging Early Interests

While the recruitment of college women to fields such as engineering and science is certainly worth exploration and experimentation, I am inclined to think that most such efforts will fail.

By the time women reach college age, most of them have been programmed out of scientific careers—and not only by the discouragement they may have received from family and peers. Another vitally important factor is the failure of most women to develop any real interests in these fields.

Although career choice in general is relatively unstable, scientists tend to develop an interest in science early in life. In boys, this develops as early as the sixth or seventh grade. Women scientists are more likely to trace the origin of their interest to a high school or junior high school teacher. In other words, boys appear to be encouraged *at home* to follow scientific interests, while girls, lacking this early impetus, must obtain it later from teachers if they are to do so at all. Of course, a few girls do receive encouragement at home.

The life histories of many outstanding women provide clear documentation of the importance of this encouragement and positive influence in developing early interests. At the age of twelve, Maria Mitchell, later to become America's most famous woman astronomer, timed and recorded a solar eclipse from the widow's walk of her Nantucket home. For several years she had already been assisting her father in rating chronometers for the Nantucket whaling fleet, checking them by stellar observation.

Sarah Frances Whiting, physicist and astronomer, the first physics professor at Wellesley College, developed an avid interest in experimental science by assisting her father in preparing demonstrations for his classes in physics. Mary Jane Rathburn, an early woman zoologist and marine biologist, developed a career in zoology out of early curiosity about fossils discovered in her family's quarries. The unusual interests of Margaret E. Knight, a prolific woman inventor who patented twenty-seven devices including a machine for folding square-bottomed paper bags must have been encouraged or at least accepted by her family. She recalled that in childhood "I never cared for the things that girls usually do. The only things I wanted were a jacknife, a gimlet, and pieces of wood. I was famous for my kites, and my sleds were the envy and admiration of all the boys in town."[1]

The importance of family influences in developing interests which may lead to careers is not limited to the fields of science. Candace Thurber Wheeler, a pioneer in American textile design and founder of Associated Artists in New York, was the daughter of a Presbyterian deacon and abolitionist who encouraged her skill at drawing and her love of nature, and a mother who taught her to spin, knit, sew, and weave. She later remembered her home as the center "of a lively creative interest."[2] Edith Wharton's father taught her to read, encouraged her love of books, and provided her with tutors so that she acquired command of the language in each country where the family lived.

Edna St. Vincent Millay was brought up by a mother who supported the family by working as a practical nurse and whose unfulfilled literary ambitions prompted her to teach her daughter to write verse at the age of four. Lillian Norton Nordica, Wagnerian opera singer, was the daughter of parents who met while singing in the church choir. Everybody in the family sang, and it was taken for granted that Lillian would sing, too.

Similarly, many women who became leaders in social reform received early parental indoctrination in liberal thinking. Harriet Beecher Stowe, who wrote *Uncle Tom's Cabin* to serve the cause of abolition, was the daughter of a minister, revivalist, and moral reformer who inspired all seven of his sons to become ministers, Harriet to labor in the cause of abolition, and Catharine to found the Hartford Female Seminary.

The suffragist Susan B. Anthony was educated by her Quaker father in the tenets of that religion, including belief in the equality of women before God. Such men as Frederick Douglass, William Lloyd Garrison, and Wendell Phillips were frequent guests in the Anthony home, and Susan's interests in the reform movements of the day—temperance, antislavery, and women's rights—had their roots in these early beginnings. Jane Addams, founder of Hull House, was strongly influenced by the moral fervor of her father, a vigorous abolitionist and a friend and admirer of Lincoln. The father of Emma Willard, founder of the Middlebury Female Seminary and the Troy Female Seminary (later renamed the Emma Willard School), encouraged her to disregard the pre-

vailing opinion that girls should accept a life of intellectual inferiority. By the time she was fourteen, he was dis-
cussing philosophy with her.

However, it is perhaps in the field of science that the
role of early exposure must be stressed, since for girls it is
so often lacking. The influence of unusual, curiosity-
arousing early experiences on the development of women
science majors was pointed up in a study done during the
early sixties. One MIT graduate with a major in naval
architecture and marine engineering, working in the
research department of a company building submarines,
grew up in a marine and mechanical atmosphere. The
daughter of a builder of small boats, she was always
curious about what makes boats run, and was encouraged in this interest by her father.[3]

In one book I encountered in my search for information about the development of scientific interests, I
came across the following statement, written by a science
teacher:

> The woman of tomorrow will use more power
> machines, electronic devices, motors and scientific
> principles in home management. The mother, as she
> pursues her daily household tasks, is the girl's first
> teacher of science. Accurate explorations of the way in
> which each machine works, proper use and care of
> equipment, the physical or chemical changes taking
> place in food preparation can help your daughter to
> become a more confident and well-informed indi-
> vidual. Boys are naturally curious, and in our culture
> they are expected to be interested in mechanical
> things. Unless the mother directs the girl's obser-
> vation, answers her questions, and suggests reading
> materials, she is not likely to become interested in the
> how or why of scientific phenomena. Plants and pets
> may attract her, but physical or chemical reactions
> may have very little attraction until the teen years,
> when she takes high school physics or chemistry.[4]

If this teacher has stimulated many girls to follow scientific careers, news of it would be a great surprise to me. This book was published in 1959, but the attitudes it expresses toward women are archaic enough to have been written in 1859. And this from a *woman* science teacher!

In a series of experiments on creativity, psychologist Paul Torrance asked children to "make toys more fun to play with." Some first grade boys, already imbued with sex-role stereotypes, refused to try the nurse's kit until some of the more inventive ones first converted it into a doctor's kit. By the third grade, boys outdid girls on suggestions for improving all toys, even the nurse's kit.[5] Torrance believes that by this age girls have been conditioned to accept things as they are, without questioning or trying to change them.

Further experiments with scientific toys, using third, fourth, and fifth graders as subjects, provided additional evidence that sex-role conditioning does indeed have an inhibiting effect on creative functioning. Girls were reluctant to work with the scientific toys, explaining that girls didn't do such things.

But Torrance wanted to see whether these biases could be overcome, and asked parents and teachers in one school to cooperate with him in trying to change children's attitudes. When retested a year later, in 1960, the girls came up with as many creative suggestions as the boys. However, Torrance found that one thing hadn't changed. The boys' suggestions were valued more highly than the girls' by children of both sexes.

Torrance also reports that the highly creative boy has more feminine interests than the average boy, while the highly creative girl has more masculine interests than the average girl. This suggests that rigid sex-role stereotyping is a detriment to creativity in either sex.

Just what *is* creativity?

Torrance describes it as "the process of sensing gaps or disturbing missing elements, forming ideas or hypotheses, testing them, and communicating the results." This sounds much like the description of a scientific experiment, and in fact it is. Creativity in the arts may appear less structured but it, too, involves many of the same elements of experimentation.

Studies of National Merit Finalists have provided some concrete information about the early behaviors that are predictive of later creative performance. In the field of science, these activities include:

• Presenting an original paper at a scientific meeting sponsored by a professional society.
• Winning a prize or award in a scientific talent search.
• Constructing scientific apparatus on own initiative.
• Inventing a patentable device.
• Having a scientific paper published in a scientific journal.

In the creative arts, predictive items were found to be:

• Winning one or more speech contests.
• Having poems, stories, or articles published in publications, newspapers or magazines (not school papers) or in state or national high school anthologies.
• Winning a prize or award in an art competition (sculpture, ceramics, painting).
• Receiving the highest rating in a state music contest.
• Receiving one of the highest ratings in a national music contest.
• Composing music which had been given at least one public performance.
• Arranging music for public performances.
• Having minor roles in plays (not high school or church sponsored).
• Having leads in high school or church-sponsored plays.

- Winning literary awards or prizes for creative writing.
- Having a cartoon published in a publication, newspaper, or magazine.

These activities are admittedly the end result, and not the beginning, of considerable early experimentation and development. What can parents do to provide the optimum atmosphere for the growth of creative potential?

Creativity, like independence, flourishes best in a family atmosphere where there is little clinging and little insistence on conformity. The highly creative child often finds it difficult to conform and in fact may be described as having wild or silly ideas. The creative child or adolescent may also be somewhat estranged from peers. Torrance suggests that such children need a "sponsor" to protect them from being squelched, since their questions and answers tend to be different from those of others. Observing that most creative people have some rather obnoxious qualities, he comments that it is up to the parents of such a child to help the child become less obnoxious without sacrificing creativity. This may be easier said than done.

Even if creative children can be difficult, few parents would knowingly discourage their creativity. Most children, when they are very young, have a freshness and originality which can be seen in their imaginative play, in their stories and poems, and in their artistic work. This is often lost along the way. You can and should encourage any evidence of creativity in your daughter by directly rewarding her efforts and achievements and also by providing materials for creative, imaginative play. Paints, pencils, papers, crayons, and clay, as well as building blocks, erector sets and tinker toys, should be readily available to children of both sexes. More unusual materials for creative work, such as bits of cloth and yarn, buttons, toothpicks, straws, pipe cleaners, and all kinds of odds and ends can also provide stimulating hours of fun.

Of course, a young child who shows a particular interest or talent in art, or in music or dancing, should be given special opportunities to pursue this inclination through group classes or individual lessons. The same applies to sports. Girls who learn to swim, ski, and play tennis early are likely to carry these activities on into adulthood and to develop real proficiency. Participation in competitive sports can give your daughter the discipline of practice and training and the development and reinforcement of achievement efforts which are so essential for later success in any field—not just athletics.

If you are an expert in an area which appeals to your daughter, by all means remain actively involved in teaching her yourself even though she may be studying elsewhere as well. It will add an extra dimension of companionship to your interactions with her, and will help to solidify her interest.

Often it is difficult to know how many activities a child should be offered. I think that many suburban children are overprogrammed. Dancing school one day, swim team the next, followed by a tennis clinic, a ceramics class, Girl Scouts, church choir, and piano lessons, seems like enough to make a nervous wreck out of a child. The highest-achieving children (four in one family) I know of have been subjected to just such a regimen, yet I would not recommend it for others. In general, I think a happier balance must be found between time for relaxation and play, and programmed activities.

While enrolling your daughter in activities appropriate to her age and interests is of course important, there is something even more significant which you should strive to impart to her. I am referring to a general attitude of curiosity about the world which must be communicated from parent to child if your daughter is going to develop optimally as far as either intelligence or creativity is concerned. Since curiosity is a necessary forerunner of both creativity and the utilization of intellectual potential, it is essential to encourage your daughter's observations of nature, of mechanical things, and of everything around her, and to aid her in questioning what she sees.

Learning to observe accurately is the first step. Set an example by being actively interested in your own surroundings and letting your own curiosity guide you to new discoveries. Try to share your own knowledge with your daughter, but at the same time help her to follow inclinations of her own. If you do not know the answer to a question (and this will happen often with an intelligent child), take the time to show your daughter how to find the information she is seeking. Cultivate the habit of seeking new information for yourself when you come across a topic you would like to know more about.

There is little doubt in my mind (and probably in anybody else's, either) that a person of broad knowledge and many interests is more likely to stimulate curiosity in the young than one with more limited horizons. If you are an avid bird watcher, it will be natural for you to explain to your daughter how to distinguish a canvasback from a redhead, and to describe the territorial habits of redwings. If you are into photography, your daughter can learn about composition and exposure from you and can follow you into the darkroom to be initiated into the miracles which occur there. Such enthusiasms are often contagious, and the more of them you have, the more likely some of them are to be transmitted.

Although it pains me to say so, I'm afraid it is no accident that in most of the examples I have found of the development of strong interests in early childhood, it was the father rather than the mother who was the formative influence. Why? Undoubtedly, the worlds of most women are more restricted than those of most men. This seems to me the most likely explanation. In my experience, it appears to be most often the father who demonstrates wide knowledge and interests (not always, though!)—especially concerning mechanical and scientific matters, but frequently in politics, economics, art, and literature as well. That is why it is doubly important for fathers and other male relatives to spend as much time with their daughters as possible. If you are raising your daughter alone, I think you should make special efforts to stimulate her curiosity and to interest her in the whole world.

12

Equal Education?

Assuming you have brought up your daughter with just the right combination of warmth and encouragement, and served as the perfect model of an independent woman through your own lifestyle, so that she reaches school age free of sex-role stereotypes, what happens when she gets there?

She'll probably have a hard time.

A girl who is independent and assertive, and exhibits the traits boys are expected to show, is liable to be viewed as deviant by her teachers and peers.

This is exactly the experience reported by the twenty-five women executives in the study I have already cited.[1] Their teachers wanted them to adopt more feminine styles of behavior in play and in the classroom, but their parents uniformly upheld the child's right to be different and attempted to change the teacher's attitudes. Sometimes they succeeded. But even if they didn't, their support allowed their daughters not to conform.

I think many determined parents of independent girls will have to follow this pattern if they want to avoid the undoing of their efforts to instill feelings of competence and equality in their daughters. The truth is that teachers as a whole are a very conventional group. Often they are not even aware of the ways in which they are reinforcing cultural stereotypes.

Even at the kindergarten level, it is not unusual to find that teachers ask the boys to move desks and chairs to a different arrangement while girls sit and watch, learning to be ladies who enjoy being waited on. And when activities are arranged with students in charge, boys are usually given the primary responsibility with girls assisting—perhaps as secretaries.

Recently a team of investigators went into fifteen pre-school classes at four schools, including three private nursery schools and one privately operated day-care center, to see whether teachers treated boys and girls differently.[2] They found that the differences they observed were far greater than what would be expected by chance.

What were these differences?

When boys hit or broke things, the teachers were three times as likely to respond than if a girl did the same thing. Boys received a loud public reprimand for such behavior, but a girl who did exactly the same thing got a "brief, soft rebuke" that others weren't likely to hear. Thus boys were obtaining strong reinforcement for aggressive actions.

Girls, on the other hand, were reinforced for clinging, dependent behavior. If they stood within arm's reach of the teacher, she would talk with them or touch them affectionately. When boys were near the teachers, they would be given directions for doing things on their own.

Teachers also responded differentially to academic efforts by boys and girls. Every one of the fifteen teachers gave more physical and verbal rewards to boys who were working at intellectual tasks, and gave boys individual instruction on how to do things twice as often as they gave such attention to girls.

In one episode which was reported, a teacher was helping the children make party baskets. She worked individually with each child while stapling the handles on the baskets. On the boys' turns, she held the stapler in place while the child stapled it. But if a girl didn't spontaneously reach for the stapler when it was her turn, the teacher stapled it for her and handed it back.

Another teacher was demonstrating to two boys and a girl that water, when poured from a tall thin beaker into a short fat one, is still the same amount (Piaget's classic "conservation" experiment). When the teacher asked one of the boys to pour the water himself, the girl requested a turn and was told she would have to wait. Then the teacher let the second boy pour it and put the materials away, without giving the girl an opportunity.

The only deviation from the general finding—that teachers pay more attention to boys—was when sex-typed feminine activities, such as cooking, were involved. Even in these cases, the boys received more individualized, detailed instructions.

Of course, some teachers are exceptions.

About 250 of the exceptions gathered in late 1974 at Old Westbury College, State University of New York, for a conference on sexism in the schools sponsored by the Feminist Press.[3]

The majority of the conference participants were individual teachers who paid their own way to come from points as distant as Winnipeg, Canada, to have an opportunity to share ideas and information with others who shared their concerns about breaking down sex-role stereotypes in the classroom.

One teacher reported that she had successfully taught boys and girls to sew and to use jig saws, "all in the name of making Christmas presents." There was an acknowledged feeling among the participants that to accomplish their goals they must avoid antagonizing the traditionalists too much.

Jacqueline Clement, assistant superintendent of schools in Hanover, N.H., and one of the few educational administrators attending the conference, warned against being overly optimistic. "Ninety percent of the superintendents and teachers in the country have no idea what we're talking about," she said. "You're not dealing with people who have any awareness of the issue—except as a joke." And it's hard to change teachers' and administrators' attitudes.

The experience of many junior high and high school girls in New York was reported several years ago in a pamphlet prepared by the New York City chapter of NOW. Some of the items from the report are as follows:[4]

> Well, within my physics class last year, our teacher asked if there was anybody interested in being a lab assistant, in the physics lab, and when I raised my hand, he told all the girls to put their hands down because he was only interested in working with boys.

> There is an Honor Guard . . . students who, instead of participating in gym for the term, are monitors in the hall, and I asked my gym teacher if I could be on the Honor Guard Squad. She said it was only open to boys. I then went to the head of the Honor Guard . . . who said that he thought girls were much too nasty to be Honor Guards. He thought they would be too mean in working on the job, and I left it at that.

> We asked for basketball. They said there wasn't enough equipment. The boys prefer to have it first. Then we will have what is left over. We haven't really gotten anywhere.

Here is a more extensive quote from one case:

> MOTHER: I asked Miss Jonas if my daughter could take metalworking or mechanics, and she said there is no freedom of choice. That is what she said.
>
> THE COURT: That is it?
>
> ANSWER: I also asked her whose decision this was, that there was no freedom of choice. And she told me it was the decision of the board of education. I didn't ask her anything else because she clearly showed me that it was against the school policy for girls to be in the class. She said it was a board of education decision.
>
> QUESTION: Did she use that phrase, "no freedom of choice?"
>
> ANSWER: Exactly that phrase—no freedom of choice. That is what made me so angry that I wanted to start this whole thing.

● ● ● ● ●

> THE COURT: Now, after this lawsuit was filed, they then permitted you to take the course; is that correct?
>
> DAUGHTER: No, we had to fight about it for quite a while.
>
> QUESTION: But eventually they did let you in the second semester?
>
> ANSWER: They only let me in there.
>
> Q. You are the only girl?
>
> A. Yes.
>
> Q. How did you do in the course?
>
> A. I got the medal for it from all the boys there.
>
> Q. Will you show the court?
>
> A. Yes (indicating).
>
> Q. And what does the medal say?
>
> A. Metal 1970 Van Syck.
>
> Q. And why did they give you that medal?
>
> A. Because I was the best one out of all the boys.

In some cases, schools have responded to the increasing pressure for sexual equality by making formerly sex-typed courses available or compulsory for children of both sexes.

And occasionally this has produced startling results. In New Milford, Conn., two Baptist ministers threatened court action against the school board's 1974 decision to make shop and home economics classes mandatory for both boys and girls.

"By having a young boy cook or sew, wearing aprons, we're pushing a boy into homosexuality," one of the ministers insisted. "It's contrary to what the home and the Bible have stood for. When God set up the human race, there was a division of the sexes . . . A woman's place is in the home, and that's where God put them, barring unusual circumstances."[5]

Fortunately, the school board did not take the complaints seriously, but they did excuse the minister's son from taking home economics "for religious reasons."

Not only do teachers often perpetuate sex-role stereotypes—peer pressure is strong, too, and most of it is in the direction of cultural conformity.

When Harvard psychologist Marcia Guttentag and a team of researchers set up a six-week curriculum designed to raise the consciousness of over 1,000 children in three age groups (kindergarten, fifth grade, and ninth grade) in three large, ethnically diverse school districts in Boston, they found—as expected—that most of the children were "ripe old sexists" by age five.[6] The children thought boys were strong and capable of many interesting jobs, but viewed girls as weak and silly.

Children of all ages viewed women as having more restricted job possibilities than men. At the end of the program, girls of all ages demonstrated considerably broader views of the possibilites open to them, but boys had shifted to an even more traditional position than they held originally. It didn't seem to matter whether the boys had working mothers or not, or whether the working mothers were waitresses or doctors. It seemed that peer group pressure, for the boys, was stronger than the example they had seen at home.

The fact is that despite statistics which clearly tell us half of all mothers in the United States are working, the example of a working mother may be overpowered by a constant barrage of information about helpless, home-bound women on TV and in school books. The child of a working mother may just conclude that her (or his) mother must be different somehow from the *real* mothers, who may always be found at home baking cookies or pushing a cart around the supermarket.

Dr. Leonare J. Weitzman, professor of sociology at the University of California, recently completed a two-year study of the most popular text books used in grades one to six across the United States.[7] Some of the highlights of her study were:

> Motherhood is shown as the only choice for girls. Throughout the texts girls are shown sewing, baking, mopping, making beds, dusting, and washing dishes.
>
> Pictures showing boys and girls together frequently show the boy doing something interesting and the girl watching.
>
> Most pictures portray girls as passive and boys as active and adventurous; girls indoors, boys outdoors.
>
> Girls are shown as affectionate, easily frightened and crying frequently, while boys are portrayed as strong, silent, and seldom crying.
>
> Spelling books used by 75 percent of the nation's elementary pupils reflect a strong sex bias, many showing the vowels as puppets in female clothing and the consonants as males pulling the strings. Female figures are yelled at and pushed around by the male figures.

"After studying these textbooks for two years we cannot help but conclude that your children are being crippled by the latent messages of these books," Dr. Weitzman stated.

Among the illustrations in one fifth grade arithmetic textbook were the following:

1. boys playing marbles; girls sewing.
2. boys earning money, building things, and going places; girls buying ribbons for a sewing project.
3. boys working at physical activities; girls baby-sitting and sewing.

In another math text, the investigators found problems in which girls were paid less than boys for doing the same work.

A recent catalogue of children's books, distributed by the National Council of Teachers of English, described the heroines of books listed under the heading "Especially for Girls" as "overcoming difficulties," "feeling lost," "helping solve" and "helping (someone) out." Not surprisingly, heroes of the books "Especially for Boys" were "deciphering and discovering," "earning and training," and "foiling" someone. The boys in these books are active and capable, the girls passive and dependent.

What can you, as a parent, do to combat the insidious influences your child is probably being exposed to?

I think you can approach the situation on two levels.

First, you should become aware, through a careful examination of the books your child is using at school, and through visiting the classroom, of exactly what she is being taught. If you feel that stereotypes are being promoted by the school, the teacher or the books being used, it is your right to speak up assertively about your feelings. You should take the role of your daughter's protector as did the parents of those twenty-five successful women executives I spoke about earlier, who objected when their child's first grade teacher wanted them to be obedient, docile, and ladylike.

Second, I think you should try to initiate some action at a group level by informing other parents of your findings. Perhaps you can initiate a local committee to study the books in use at your daughter's school, and use the results as a lever for bringing about change. If you can become involved through the PTA or as a member of the school board, your efforts may be more successful.

Remember that there is strength in numbers. But don't be afraid to act as an individual whenever necessary.

13

Adolescent Conflicts about Success

During adolescence, significant sex differences in academic achievement begin to appear.

In the early school years, standardized achievement tests do not show sex differences. According to a recent $30 million assessment program, financed by the federal government, the sexes show equal achievement in math, science, social science, and citizenship until age nine. Girls still surpass boys in reading and knowledge of literature at this age.

By age thirteen, girls begin a relative decline in achievement, particularly in math and science, that continues through adulthood. When they reach the twenty-six to thirty-five age range, women trail men even in reading and knowledge of literature.[1]

These differences cannot be explained by variations in innate aptitude. In the early years, tests of intelligence show few differences between the sexes. (One source of

121

confusion in interpreting these results is that most tests were deliberately balanced to avoid sex differences.) Girls do somewhat better on verbal tests from the age of about ten through high school. Tests of mathematical ability favor boys from the age of nine, and males move steadily ahead from that point on.[2] On the Scholastic Aptitude Test, boys score an average of fifty points higher on the math section while girls fare only eight to ten points better on the verbal tests.[3]

Boys also do better on tests of spatial ability during elementary school and thus enter adolescence with a style of thinking more appropriate to scientific work than do girls. As reported in an earlier chapter, the development of math and spatial abilities are significantly related to independence training in childhood. Girls who receive this kind of training also develop the ability for analytical thinking.[4]

Not only do fewer females enter adolescence with well-developed mathematical abilities, but relatively fewer survive the rigors of high school math. A recent survey of the entering class at Berkeley in 1973 found that 57 percent of the males presented four years of high school math, compared to 8 percent of entering females. Thus 95 percent of the freshmen women were not even eligible to take calculus or any intermediate level statistics course.[5]

Math anxiety may strike at sixth grade, with the introduction to algebra, or in calculus or statistics. The malady attacks many more females than males and results in a serious block. According to Wesleyan University provost Sheila Tobias, math anxiety is "handed down from mother or daughter with father's amused indulgence."[6]

Some "mathophobics" are daughters of math professors or engineers, who may be trying very hard not to identify with their fathers. Or they may be succumbing to peer group influences. During elementary school, girls tend to think girls do better in all subjects, while boys think boys do better. By high school age, both boys and girls think boys do better in math. When a girl does poorly on a math test, she often says she doesn't have the ability to do well, while a boy who does poorly will say he didn't study hard enough.

Teachers reinforce these views. High school teachers of math, both male and female, believe that boys do better in math than girls.

Even when girls do demonstrate ability in math and science, they are less likely to be encouraged to enter competitive fields like medicine, science, or engineering. They are more often encouraged to enter nursing. In a survey of women architecture students recently, most answered that the greatest obstacle to entering architecture school was their high school counselor.[7]

Sexism is also rampant in high school vocational education programs, where women make up about half the enrollment but only one fourth the enrollment in courses leading to employment. Half the female students are in consumer and homemaking courses, and those who are in employment-related programs are concentrated in fields leading to poorly paid positions. Three fifths are training for clerical or secretarial jobs.

Title II of the Educational Amendments of 1976, signed by President Ford in October, required recipients of federal funds to initiate programs abolishing sex discriminatory practices by October 1977, with the goal of making all courses accessible to everyone.[8]

"Fear of success," the incapacitating fear of undesirable social consequences identified by Radcliffe president Matina Horner, also strikes during adolescence. Not only do girls show much more fear of success than do boys, but there is a marked and progressive increase from junior to senior high school and from the freshman to

senior years in college. An increasing percentage of girls
express fear-of-success imagery in the stories told in
response to verbal cues, whether the cues involve success
in a male dominated field or in the writing of a novel in
one's spare time.[9]

During college, many academically able girls who
show fear of success change their ambitious career plans
to safer, more traditional goals such as social work,
teaching, and nursing. Girls who are most likely to show
fear of success are those who are not dating, or whose boy
friends show disapproval of achieving women and communicate their belief that "Woman's place is in the
home." When asked how the boys in their lives react to
their ambitions, such girls often reply, "They laugh."

The evidence seems to indicate that before adolescence
girls, as well as boys, are rewarded for academic achievement and can even compete in athletics without ex-
periencing negative consequences. Being successful
academically and feeling competent and competitive are
not perceived as antifeminine in the early years.

With the onset of puberty, everything changes. Sud-
denly the competition is focused not on achievement in
school but on success in dating. And the message comes
across loud and clear that success in these two spheres is
not compatible. It is rare for the girl who is head of her
class to also be the homecoming queen. Faced with a
dichotomous choice between achievement and popularity, most adolescent girls opt for popularity. A minority
of girls flaunts cultural expectations and continues striving for achievement, but few of these escape nagging
doubts about their femininity. The majority—who may
never have been as assertive or independent as their male
peers—decide not to compete at all but to rely on others
for their sense of esteem.

In a way this is nothing new since most girls are socialized to value love and esteem from others, while boys are
encouraged to develop internal standards of perfor-

mance. At adolescence, most girls continue to base their self-esteem on their relationships with others, but now the approval is sought not only from parents but from their opposite sex peers.

In a large scale study of girls and boys aged fourteen to sixteen, subjects were asked to tell stories in response to projective pictures involving such situations as a parent setting limits for a child. When asked to tell what the child would say, a fourth of the boys questioned the parental restriction, but only 4 percent of the girls did so.[10] Boys at this age seem to be actively working toward establishing their own controls and on forming definite personal standards and values. The well-adjusted adolescent boy is actively striving for achievement, makes independent judgments, and has self-confidence yet views himself relatively realistically.

This is not true for girls. For the adolescent female, remaining dependent and compliant and showing relatively little tendency to develop personal standards and values is not only acceptable, but encouraged.

The tendency for girls to rely on external cues for self-definition is probably reinforced by the physiological changes of puberty. While a boy also experiences unfamiliar sexual impulses, he is familiar with his sexual organs and sexual excitation produces the observable external events of erection and ejaculation. In girls the experience is much more ambiguous and diffuse.

In boys, the changes of puberty occur only once. But with the onset of menstruation, widely viewed as "the curse," girls experience emotional changes on a monthly basis which they frequently do not associate with their monthly cycle—but which are in fact related. In summarizing the evidence on this point, Douvan comments that while a large majority of high school and college girls experience radical emotional shifts accompanying premenstrual hormonal changes, only about 10 percent realize that these changes are related to their menstrual cycle.[11] A girl who does not make this connection is likely to feel that she is at the mercy of forces she does not understand. It is difficult to develop a sense of internal control under such circumstances.

The net result of societal pressures toward dating and popularity, combined with the physiological changes of puberty, is that for most girls the crucial task of adolescence—viewed by most psychologists as the resolution of the identity crisis—is not accomplished.

While for males adolescence is a period of active striving toward the development of a personal identity through testing new skills, forming personal standards and values, and selecting an occupational role which will allow integration of the self-concept and provide objective measures of self-worth, the exact opposite often occurs in females. Rather than establish definite likes, dislikes, standards, and values *which will restrict her choice of a mate*, a girl is likely to avoid the resolution of her own identity. As Douvan points out, females tend to feel they must "remain fluid and malleable in personal identity in order to adapt to the needs of the men they marry."[12] Thus the important identity question remains unanswered. Many women do not begin to resolve this problem until the forties and fifties after the work of child rearing is largely completed and personal needs, as opposed to maternal and wifely demands, must finally be faced.

How can a parent help a daughter deal successfully and effectively with these adolescent conflicts?

This is no simple matter. If the groundwork has been laid in earlier years through independence training and encouragement toward achievement and autonomy, a girl is more likely to withstand the pressures of her peers and society in general which push her toward acceptance of the traditional feminine role. It is particularly important to avoid pressuring a girl into early dating and to avoid the implication that marriage and childbearing are the most important parts of her life. At the same time, she will be feeling these conflicts and should be encouraged to express them.

Many parents actually advise girls to "act dumb" in order to attract boys. I would certainly counsel against this. I would do all I could to acquaint adolescent girls with the importance of career planning and its role in life satisfaction—not just the frequently mentioned "something to fall back on." But unless other factors are strong—a father's influence or the model of a female teacher or family friend—a girl is more likely to follow her mother's example.

You should do all you can to communicate the idea that many choices are possible, including not getting married, or getting married and not having children.

And you should actively encourage your daughter to form her own standards, develop her own interests, and use her capacity for making independent judgments.

Adolescent girls also need to be informed about the mood changes which accompany their menstrual cycle so they can understand that these are biologically caused rather than see themselves as the helpless victims of external events. I was recently consulted by a young woman in her twenties who related that she had been moody as a teenager and since her marriage at twenty-one had been subject to recurrent fits of depression over which she had no control. She could not understand what was wrong as there seemed to be no external reason for her moods. When I discovered that she had been taking birth control pills since her marriage, and had her change to another form of contraception, her depressions ceased. Hormonal factors are extremely important in emotional states, and an understanding of this can be extremely helpful to a young girl. Charting daily moods in relation to the menstrual cycle can quickly demonstrate whether or not this is the case with your daughter.

14

College and Coeducation

The returns are not in yet on coeducation.

Though it has been several years since Yale, Prince
ton, Dartmouth, and many other leading men's colleges
opened their doors to women, the long-term results will
not be known for several decades.

I am, of course, speaking of the results in terms of the
achievements of their women graduates. In the past few
years, these newly co-ed schools have attracted a large
percentage of the nation's brightest young women—who
formerly would have attended Wellesley, Smith, or Mt.
Holyoke.

Perhaps Yale, Princeton, and Dartmouth are expect-
ing more of their women graduates than that they be the
well-educated wives of their male graduates, and are
providing an atmosphere in which young women can be
trained for future professional, intellectual, and economic leadership.

As recently as 1970, though, the college newspaper at
Radcliffe published the text of a purloined letter written
by the Dean of Freshmen at Harvard, who said "Quite
simply, I do not see highly educated women making
startling strides in contributing to our society in the fore-
seeable future. They are not, in my opinion, going to
stop getting married and/or having children. They will
fail in their present role as women if they do." And in
1972, a vice president at Harvard told a young woman
who had just been accepted at Harvard Law School to
"Forget this career stuff; in ten years you'll be just like
my wife . . . living in the suburbs with three kids."[1] Why
should the dean or the vice president at Yale or Princeton feel any differently?

Jill Ker Conway, who became president of Smith College in 1975, dismisses as nonsense the assumption that
simply putting women in the same classroom with men
"puts them in touch with the same resources."[2] She believes that women are treated as marginal to the male
group.

One student, who transferred to Smith from Colgate (a
former all-male school), commented: "I didn't feel that
women at Colgate were treated like first class citizens. I
wanted to be a pioneer, one of the first women at Colgate, but not for four years. Now, coming to Smith, a
school that cares about me as a woman, I get a different
sense of my self-worth. . . . At Colgate much of the
social life centered around the fraternities, so I got the
feeling that the women were there for the men's enter-
tainment. And the swimming pool, for example, was
open to men during prime hours, and to women during
dinner, so that they missed dinner if they wanted to
swim."[3]

Another Smith student, after visiting a male friend at
Dartmouth, reported: "I would never go to Dartmouth.
The men there divide the women into two categories: the

smart ones and the sex objects. They don't want to date
the smart ones."

It is a well-known fact that on co-ed campuses, a large
majority of class presidencies, editorships, and other
major posts are held by men. When men were first
accepted at Sarah Lawrence, they rapidly took over most
top student positions. As one Wellesley student put it:
"At a co-ed school, men pretty much run everything.
Maybe it's society, but you're taught to sit back and let
the men do it. Here it's different. All the leaders and doers
are women."[4]

A 1974 Carnegie Commission on Higher Education report stated that in addition to holding more leadership
positions, women students at women's colleges speak up
more in class and more frequently choose to enter science
and other traditionally male fields.[5]

Dr. Elizabeth Tidball, a professor of physiology at the
George Washington University Medical Center, studied a
representative sample of women listed in *Who's Who of
American Women*, 1966–1971, and concluded that graduates of women's colleges were more than twice as
likely to be cited for career achievement as were women
graduates of coeducational colleges.[6] This was true both
of highly selective and less selective women's colleges, so
the difference was not due to an initial selection factor. In
fact, the less selective women's colleges graduated proportionately as many achievers as did the most selective
coeducational colleges.

One factor which appeared to be important was the
ratio of women faculty to women students. The greater
the women-faculty/women-student ratio, the greater the
number of women graduates who subsequently achieve.
Women teachers as role models thus provide a crucial
element in a college environment which turns out
women achievers. The relationship between male students and women achievers was just the opposite: the

greater the proportion of male students, the fewer the women achievers. This would seem to indicate that men's colleges which have gone co-ed but remained largely male will provide an especially poor milieu for developing the talents of their women students.

For both co-ed and women's colleges, all unmarried graduates were seven times more likely to be listed in *Who's Who* than those who were married. The proportion of married achievers was the same—57 percent—for both co-ed and women's colleges. But the married graduates of women's colleges were almost three times as likely to be listed as were married women graduates of co-educational colleges.

Most successful career women report the active encouragement and interest of a faculty member in their future work. This seems more likely to occur in the setting of a women's college where a promising young woman student need not outdistance her male competitors in order to be noticed. While at Wellesley, I was actively encouraged by two professors—both of whom happened to be male. Recently I heard Sheila Tobias, historian and Wesleyan University Provost, remark that Harvard had managed to give her both a Phi Beta Kappa key and a feeling that she was a second-class citizen. She said that no faculty member had singled her out for special recognition or encouragement. I felt glad that I had gone to Wellesley. After more than twenty-five years, I still correspond with one of my professors and with the widow of another who died a few years ago.

Wellesley did not make me feel second-class. On the other hand, my classmates and I received relatively little help or preparation at Wellesley for the struggles that would lie ahead. Like the other leading women's colleges, Wellesley has not met the feminist challenge of preparing women for important roles in the world beyond those of scholarship and motherhood. On the whole, the women's colleges have not taught their students to be assertive and independent, but have more or less perpetuated traditional stereotypes. As Nora Ephron, a Wellesley graduate, put it: "The class deans . . . were a group of elderly spinsters who believed that the only valuable role for Wellesley graduates was to go on to the only life the deans knew anything about—graduate school, scholarship, teaching. There was no value at all placed on achievement in the so-called real world. Success of this sort was suspect. Worse than that, it was unserious. Better to be a housewife, my dear, and to take one's place in the community."[7]

Jill Ker Conway, who hopes to integrate courses in accounting and business management with the existing curriculum at Smith, comments that "The whole structure of higher education for women was built without any attempt to relate the educated person to the occupational structure of society outside. That's why the whole first generation of educated women had nervous collapses."[8]

The last few years have seen an upswing in applications for admission to women's colleges. Since 1971, when applications to many reached an all time low and many others closed their doors, the pendulum has swung around again. By 1973, 51 percent of the women's colleges responding to an Association of American Colleges questionnaire reported an increase in applications, with 21 percent holding their own from the prior year's level.[9] Wellesley received a record number of applications for its freshman class of 1975, as did Mt. Holyoke.[10]

There are, of course, two sides to every question. Students and educators who favor coeducation believe that segregating women during the college years is only postponing the time when they will have to enter the real world and compete with men as well as women. A recent

editorial in the Smith College newspaper, *The Sophian,*
claimed that "Smith is isolating and protecting women
from reality. Smith is teaching us to fear, distrust, and
idolize men, instead of teaching us to deal with them as
equals. During some of the most impressionable years of
our lives, it is wrong to be isolated from one half of the
human race. Only through mutual understanding will
'the feminine mystique' be dispelled. We know we are
not naturally docile and stupid, but the environment
here nurtures these attitudes."

My oldest daughter, an architectural student at the
Rhode Island School of Design, wanted nothing to do
with women's colleges and spent her first two years of
college at the University of Pennsylvania. My middle
daughter is a student at Smith. My youngest plans to
attend Yale.

If you have raised your daughter to be assertive and independent, the choice of what college she attends will be
a choice she makes herself based on her own values and
future plans. There will be relatively little you can do to
influence her choice, but you can acquaint her with the
positive advantages of a women's college and urge her to
visit at least one before she makes her final decision.

There is no one right choice for everyone. A girl who
knows while still in high school that she wants a career
in engineering or architecture will not find what she
needs in a women's college.

Too often, young women choose a college without
asking whether its graduates attain the kind of success
she is seeking for herself. I think this is an issue which
should be carefully considered when it is time to make
this decision. And most of the facts available to date indicate that the women's colleges have been considerably
more effective in producing women of achievement than
have their coeducational counterparts.

Notes &
References

Chapter 1:
What Is a Successful Daughter

1. U.S. Bureau of the Census.
2. Kundsin, R. B. (Ed.) *Women and success*. New York: William Morrow and Co., 1974.
3. Horner, M. Femininity and successful achievement: a basic inconsistency. In E. L. Walker (Ed.) *Feminine personality and conflict*. Belmont, Calif.: Brooks/Cole Publishing Co., 1970.
4. Broverman, I. K., Broverman, D. M., Clarkson, F. E., Rosenkrantz, P. S., and Vogel, S. R. Sex-role stereotypes and clinical judgments of mental health. *Journal of Consulting and Clinical Psychology*, 34:1 (1970): 1-7.

Chapter 2:
A Forecast of Your Daughter's Life

1. U.S. Department of Labor, Women's Bureau.
2. Bailyn, L. Family constraints on women's work. In R. B. Kundsin (Ed.). *Women and success*. New York: William Morrow and Co., 1974. Pp. 94-102.
3. Hoffman, L. W. The professional woman as mother. In Kundsin. *Women and success*. Pp. 222-28.
4. U.S. Department of Commerce, Bureau of the Census, Current Population Reports, Series P 20, No. 298.
5. Janeway, E. *Between myth and morning: women awakening*. New York: William Morrow and Co., 1974.
6. Langner, T. S., and Michael, S. T. *Life stress and mental health*. New York: Macmillan, 1963.
7. LeMasters, E. E. Parenthood as crisis. *Marriage and family living*, 19, (1957): 352-55.
8. Birnbaum, J. Life patterns, personality style and self-esteem in gifted family oriented and career committed women. Doctoral dissertation, University of Michigan, 1971.

9. U.S. Bureau of the Census, Census of Population, 1970.
10. U.S. Bureau of the Census.
11. Sufer, L. E., and Miller, H. P. Income differences between men and career women. In J. Huber (Ed.). *Changing women in a changing society.* Chicago: University of Chicago Press, 1973. Pp. 200–212.
12. Oppenheimer, V. K. Demographic influence on female employment. In Huber. *Changing women in a changing society.* Pp. 184–89.
13. Astin, H. S. *The woman doctorate in America: origins, career, and family.* New York: The Russell Sage Foundation, 1969.
14. Holhstrom, L. L. *The two-career family.* Cambridge: Schenkman Publishing Company, 1973.

Chapter 3:
Avoiding Sexual Stereotypes

1. Will, J. Z., Provenzana, F. J., and Luria, Z. The eye of the beholder: parents' views on sex of newborns. *American Journal of Orthopsychiatry*, 44 (4) (July 1974).
2. Moss, H. A. Sex, age, and state as determinants of mother-infant interaction. In J. M. Bardwick (Ed.). *Readings on the psychology of women.* New York: Harper and Row, 1972. Pp. 22–29.
3. Goldberg, S., and Lewis, M. Play behavior in the year-old infant: early sex differences. In J. M. Bardwick (Ed.). *Reading on the psychology of women.* New York: Harper and Row, 1972.
4. Will, J. A., Self, P., and Datan, N., Maternal behavior and sex of infant. Unpublished paper.
5. Hartley, R. D. A developmental view of female sex-role definition and identification. *Merrill-Palmer Quarterly of behavior and development.* 10 (1964): 3–16
6. Hartup, W. W., and Sook, E. D. Sex role preferences in three and four year old children. *Journal of Consulting Psychology*, 24 (1960): 420–26.
7. Spock, B. J. *Spock Talks to mothers.* Boston: Houghton-Mifflin, 1961.
8. Cited in Howe, F. Sexual stereotypes start early. *Saturday Review*, October 16, 1971.
9. Rossi, A. Barriers to the career choice of engineering, medicine, or science among American women. In Bardwick. *Readings on the psychology of women.*
10. Women engineers, *Parade*, February 9, 1975.
11. Hennig, M. M. Family dynamics and the successful woman executive. In R. B. Kundsin (Ed.). *Women and success.* New York: William Morrow and Co., 1974.

Chapter 4:
Building Self-Confidence

1. Goldberg, P. A. Are women prejudiced against women? *Trans-Action* (1968): 28–30.

2. Gurin, F., Veroff, J., and Feld, S. *Americans view their mental health.* New York: Basic Books, 1960; Bradburn, N. M., and Caplovitz, D. *Reports on happiness.* Chicago: Aldine, 1969.
3. Rossi, A. Transition to parenthood. *Journal of Marriage and the Family,* XXX (1968): 26–39.
4. Birnbaum, J. Life patterns, personality style and self-esteem in gifted family oriented and career committed women. Doctoral dissertation, University of Michigan, 1971.
5. Martinson, F. M. Ego deficiency as a factor in marriage. *American Sociological Review,* 20 (April 1955): 161–64.
6. Ross, D. R. The story of the top 1% of the women at Michigan State University, 1963 (Mimeograph).

Chapter 5:
Developing Independence

1. Newson, J., and Newson, E. Four years old in an urban community. Harmondworth, England: Pelican Books, 1968; cited in E. E. Maccoby and C. N. Jacklin. *The psychology of sex differences.* Stanford, Calif.: Stanford University Press, 1974.
2. White, B. L., and Watts, J. C. *Experience and environment.* Englewood Cliffs, N.J.: Prentice-Hall, 1973.
3. Levy, D. M. *Maternal overprotection.* New York: Columbia University Press, 1943.
4. Maccoby, E. E., and Rau, L. *Differential cognitive abilities.* Final report, cooperative research project No. 1040. Stanford, Calif.: Owen House, Stanford University, 1962; cited in E. E. Maccoby. Woman's intellect. In S. M. Farber and R. H. L. Wilson (Eds.). *The potential of women.* New York: McGraw-Hill, 1963.
5. Maccoby. Woman's intellect.
6. Ibid.
7. James, E. T., James, J. W., and Boyer, P. S. (Eds,). *Notable American women.* Cambridge, Mass.: Harvard University Press, 1971.
8. Rossi, A. Barriers to the career choice of engineering, medicine, or science among American women. In J. A. Mattfeld and C. G. Van Aken (Eds.). *Women and the scientific professions.* Cambridge: The M.I.T. Press, 1965.

Chapter 6:
Enhancing Achievement Efforts

1. Horner, M. Femininity and successful achievement: a basic inconsistency. In E. L. Walker (Ed.). *Feminine personality and conflict.* Belmont, Calif.: Brooks/Cole Publishing Co. 1970.
2. Ibid.
3. Alper, T. G. Achievement motivation in college women: a now-you-see-it-now-you-don't phenomenon. *American Psychologist,* 29, 3 (March 1974): 194–203.

4. Crandall, V. J., Preston, A., and Rabson, A. Maternal reactions and the development of independence and achievement behavior in young children. *Child Development*, 31 (1960): 243–51.
5. Stein, A. H., and Bailey, M. M. The socialization of achievement orientation in females. *Psychological Bulletin*, 80, 5 (1973): 345–65.

Chapter 7:
Providing Role Models

1. Almquist, E. M., and Angrist, S. S. Role model influences on college women's career aspirations. *Merrill-Palmer Quarterly*, (1971): 263–79.
2. Padan, D. Intergenerational mobility of women: a two-step process of status mobility in a context of a value conflict, 1965. Publication of Tel Aviv University, Tel Aviv, Israel; cited in Lozoff, M. M. Fathers and autonomy in women. In R. B. Kundsin (Ed.). *Women and success*. New York: William Morrow and Co., 1974.
3. Birnbaum, J. Life patterns, personality style and self-esteem in gifted family oriented and career committed women. Doctoral dissertation, The University of Michigan, 1971.
4. Ginzberg, E. *Educated American women: life styles and self-portraits*. New York: Columbia University Press, 1966.
5. Ibid.
6. McIntosh, M. Educator. In Kundsin. *Women and success*.
7. Powell, B. *Careers for women after marriage and children*. New York: Macmillan, 1965.

Chapter 9:
Fathers and Daughters

1. Lozoff, M. M. Fathers and autonomy in women. In R. B. Kundsin (Ed.). *Women and success*. New York: William Morrow and Co., 1974.
2. Birnbaum, J. Life patterns, personality style and self-esteem in gifted family oriented and career committed women. Doctoral dissertation, The University of Michigan, 1971.
3. Hennig, M. M. Family dynamics and the successful woman executive. In Kundsin. *Women and success*.

Chapter 10:
Having a Small Family

1. Altus, W. D. Birth order and its sequelae. *Science*, vol. 151 (January 1966).
2. Hennig, M. M. Family dynamics and the successful woman executive. In R. B. Kundsin (Ed.). *Women and success*. New York: William Morrow and Co., 1974.
3. Anderson, J. V. Psychological determinants. In Kundsin. *Women and success*.
4. Altus. Birth order and its sequelae.
5. Ibid.

6. Belmont, L., and Marolla, F. A. Birth order, family size, and intelligence. *Science*, vol. 182 (December 1973).
7. Altus. Birth order and its sequelae.
8. Zajonc, R. B. Dumber by the dozen. *Psychology Today*, January 1975.

Chapter 11:
Encouraging Early Interests

1. James, E. T., James, J. W., and Boyer, P. S., Eds. *Notable American women*. Cambridge, Mass.: Harvard University Press, 1971.
2. Ibid.
3. Dement, A. L. What brings and holds women science majors. *College and University*, 39, no. 1 (Fall 1963).
4. Weinlander, Albertina A. *Your child in a scientific world*. New York: Doubleday, 1959.
5. Torrance, E. P. *Guiding creative talent*. Englewood Cliffs, N.J.: Prentice-Hall, 1962.

Chapter 12:
Equal Education?

1. Hennig, M. M. Family dynamics and the successful woman executive. In R. B. Kundsin (Ed.). *Women and success: the anatomy of achievement*. New York: William Morrow and Company, 1974.
2. Serbin, L. A., and O'Leary, K. D. How nursery schools teach girls to shut up. *Psychology Today*, December 1975.
3. Hammel, L. Teachers meet to fight sexism in the schools. *New York Times*, November 25, 1974.
4. Cited by Howe, F. Sexual stereotypes start early. *Saturday Review*, October 16, 1971.
5. Knight, M. Two ministers threaten suit over boys' cooking classes. *New York Times*, December 5, 1974.
6. Cited by Serbin and O'Leary. How nursery schools teach girls to shut up.
7. McCormack, P. Spelling texts reflect antagonism toward girls, woman's study says. UPI, *Bridgeport Sunday Post*, December 15, 1974.

Chapter 13:
Adolescent Conflicts about Success

1. Maeroff, G. Tests find males excel in academic attainment. *New York Times*, October 13, 1975.
2. Maccoby, E. E., and Jacklin, C. N. *The psychology of sex differences*. Stanford: Stanford University Press, 1974.
3. Rossi, A. Barriers to the career choice of engineering, medicine, or science among American women. In J. M. Bardwick (Ed.). *Readings on the psychology of women*. New York: Harper and Row, 1972.
4. Maccoby. The psychology of sex differences.

5. Tobias, Sheila. Math anxiety. *Ms.* September, 1976.
6. Ibid.
7. Latourell, E. D. So she wants to be an architect. *Do it Now*, June, 1976.
8. Fiske, E. B. U. S. acts to end alleged "sexism" in vocational education. *New York Times*, October 20, 1976.
9. Horner, M. S. Femininity and successful achievement: a basic inconsistency. In E. Walker (Ed.). *Feminine personality and conflict*. Belmont, Calif.: Brooks/Cole Publishing Co.
10. Douvan, E. Sex differences in adolescent character processes. In Bardwick. *Readings on the psychology of women*.
11. Douvan, E. New sources of conflict in females at adolescence and early adulthood. In Walker. *Feminine personality and conflict*.
12. Douvan. Sex differences in adolescent character processes.

Chapter 14:
College and Coeducation

1. Zinberg, D. College: when the future becomes the present. In R. B. Kundsin (Ed.) *Women and success*. New York: William Morrow and Company, 1974.
2. *New York Times*, Dr. Mattfeld takes Barnard helm as panel weighs women's options. November 6, 1976.
3. Backalenick, I. Women's colleges, yes or no? *Fairfield County*, August, 1975.
4. Brown, P. A. Despite changes, women's colleges plan to be around for some time. *Bridgeport Post* (UPI), February 16, 1976.
5. Backalenick. Women's colleges.
6. Tidball, E. The search for talented women. *Change*, May 1974.
7. Ephron, N. Reunion. In *Crazy Salad*. New York: Alfred A. Knopf, 1975.
8. Bender, M. Smith's first woman president anticipates a "great adventure." *New York Times*, March 18, 1975.
9. Backalenick. Women's colleges.
10. *Wellesley College Bulletin*, April, 1975.

Index

Achievement motivation, 55–61
Addams, Jane, 46, 78, 102
Adolescence, 121–27
Agoraphobia, 44–45
Alcott, Louisa May, 81
Altus, W. D., 93
American Men of Science, 92, 95
Anthony, Susan B., 84, 103
Austen, Jane, 7

Barton, Clara, 73, 81, 82
Beecher, Catherine, 91–92, 103
Beecher, Henry Ward, 91
Beecher, Lyman, 91
Belle of the Fifties, A, 75
Bemelmans, Ludwig, 28
Birth order, 93–99
Blackberry Winter, 67, 73
Blackwell, Antoinette Brown, 91, 93
Blackwell, Elizabeth, 73, 90, 93
Blackwell, Emily, 90–91
Blackwell, Henry, 91
Blackwell, Samuel, 90–91
Blackwell, Samuel Charles, 91
Bronte, Charlotte, 7
Bronte, Emily, 7
Brown, Antoinette Louisa
    (Blackwell), 91
Brownmiller, Susan, 73
Bryn Mawr, 51, 68
Buck, Pearl, 85

Cather, Willa, 83
Cattell, R. B., 94
*Century of Struggle: The Woman's
    Rights Movement in the United
    States*, 72
Challenge to Become a Doctor, 73
Childbirth and crisis reaction, 14
Child care arrangements. *See*
    Women, in labor force
Chopin, Kate, 79
Clay-Clopton, Virginia Tunstall, 75
Clement, Jacqueline, 114
Coeducation, 129–34
Coleman, Hila, 28
Colgate University, 130
Competence: judgments of, male vs.
    female, 37–38, 105; and
    maternal behavior, 48–49
Conway, Jill Ker, 130, 133
Country of the Pointed Firs, The, 80
Creativity, 105–9
Curie, Madame Eve, 73

Dartmouth College, 129–31
Daughter of Discontent, 28
Dictionary of National Biography,
    94
Divorce, 45–46
Doll's House, A, 74
Doty, Roy, 28
Douglass, Frederick, 103

Douvan, Elizabeth, 125-26

Earnings, women vs. men, 16
Eddy, Mary Baker, 81, 82, 83
Education, early, 113-19
Educational achievement, males vs. females, 121-23
Educational attainment and employment, 12
Eliot, George, 7
Ellis, Havelock, 94
Emma, 7
English Men of Science, 93-94
Ephron, Nora, 133

Family size, 95-99
Fathers, relationship with successful daughters, 88-92, 102-4
Fear of success, 4-7, 56, 123-24
Fearn, Anne Walter, 83
Feminine Mystique, The, 72
Fitzhugh, Louise, 28
Fleming, Alice, 73
Flexner, Eleanor, 72
Ford, President Gerald, 123
Freckles, 78
Friedan, Betty, 72

Galton, Sir Frances, 93-96
Garrison, William Lloyd, 103
Geneva College, 90
Girl of the Limberlost, A, 78
Girls Can be Anything, 28
Girl Scouts of America, 77
Glasgow, Ellen, 85
Good Earth, The, 85
Gornick, Vivian, 72
Growing Up Female in America, 73
Guttentag, Marcia, 116

Harriet the Spy, 28
Harvard University, 130, 132
Hatchett Hall, 76
Hayes, Eleanor, 72
Heyne, Leah Lurie, 73
Hooker, Isabella Beecher, 92
Horner, Matina, 4-7, 56, 123-24
Hull House, 78, 102
Husbands' encouragement and professional work, 18-19, 87

Ibsen, Henrik, 74
Independence training, 43-53
IQ, 95-99; increases during childhood, 50
Interrupted career pattern, 15
Island of the Blue Dolphins, 28
It Scale, 27

Jackson, Helen Hunt, 76
Janeway, Elizabeth, 14, 72
Jewett, Sarah Orne, 80

Keller, Helen, 73, 75-76
Knight, Margaret E., 102

Lee, Mother Ann, 80, 82
Lingren, Astrid, 28
Little Women, 81
Low, Juliette Gordon, 77
Lucretia Mott, 73

McIntosh, Millicent, 68
Madeline's Rescue, 28
Man's World, Woman's Place, 72
Marriage: and career achievement, 132; and educational attainment, 17-18; and happiness, 39; and self-confidence, 39-41
Maternal employment: and career orientation, 65-67; and guilt, 14; and judgments of women's competence, 65; and juvenile delinquency, 13
Math: anxiety, 122-23; preparation, males vs. females, 122
Mathematical ability and independence training, 49-50
Mead, Margaret, 67, 73
Menstruation, 125-27
Mental health, double standard of, 7-8, 44
Merriam, Eve, 28, 73
Middlebury Female Seminary, 84, 103
Middlemarch, 7
Millay, Edna St. Vincent, 103
Miracle Worker, The, 76
Mitchell, Maria, 51-52, 74, 82, 102
Mommies at Work, 28

Moran, Barbara K., 72
*Morningstar, a Biography of Lucy
    Stone*, 72
Mt. Holyoke College, 133
Ms. magazine, 27

Nantucket, 51–52, 74, 102
Nathan, Dorothy, 73
Nation, Carry, 76, 79
National Merit Finalists, 96, 106
Nobel prize, 78, 85
Nordica, Lillian Norton, 80, 103
Notable American Women, 74

O'Dell, Scott, 28
Only children, 93–99
Overprotectiveness and achievement
    behavior, 59

Permissiveness and achievement
    behavior, 58
Phillips, Wendell, 103
Piaget, Jean, 113
Pippi Longstocking, 28
Porter, Gene Stratton, 78–79
Portis, Charles, 28
Princeton University, 129–30
Puberty, 125–27
Pulitzer Prize, 77, 85

Quimby, Phineas, 81

Radcliffe College, 56, 130
Ramona, 76
Rathburn, Mary Jane, 102
Rawlings, Marjorie Kinnan, 77
Rhodes Scholars, 94
Roe, Anne, 49
Role models, 63–39, 131
Room of One's Own, A, 7, 72, 73
Rossi, Alice, 39

Salter, Susanna Medora, 79
Sarah Lawrence College, 131
Scholastic Aptitude Test, 122
Science of Man, The, 81
Scientific interests, origins of,
    101–10
Self-esteem, 33–41, 124–25
Senator From Maine, The, 73

Seton, Elizabeth, 80
Sex differences: in academic
    achievement, 121–22; in
    educational experiences, 111–19;
    in infancy, 23–25; in locus of
    control, 125
Sexism in schools, 111–19
Sex-role orientation, 56–57
Sex-role stereotypes: and books, 28,
    117–18; in children, 27; in
    schools, 114–19, 123; and toys,
    25–27
Sex-typing, 21, 63–64
Shaker villages, 80, 82
Shakespeare, William, 7
Shirley Chisholm, 73
Smith College, 130–31, 133, 134
Smith, Margaret Chase, 73
Sophian, The, 134
Spock, Benjamin, 28–29
Stanton, Elizabeth Cady, 29, 85
Stanwood, Cordelia, 80
Stepford Wives, The, 74
Sterling, Dorothy, 73
Stone, Lucy, 91
Stowe, Harriet Beecher, 74, 76–77,
    79, 91, 93, 103
Study of British Genius, A, 94
Success, definition of, 1–4. *See also*
    Fear of success

Teachers' treatment of males vs.
    females, 112–13
Terman, Lewis, 95
Thomas, M. Carey, 46, 51, 68
Tidball, Elizabeth, 131–32
Tobias, Sheila, 122, 132
Torrance, Paul, 105–7
Tory Lover, The, 80
Toys, 25–28
Troy Female Seminary, 84, 103
True Grit, 28
Tubman, Harriet, 83–84
Twenty Years at Hull House, 78

Uncle Tom's Cabin, 75, 79, 103

Vassar College, 52, 82
Villette, 7
Volunteer work, 3

Weitzman, Leonare, 117–18
Wellesley College, 53, 56–57, 102,
    131, 132–33
Wharton, Edith, 103
Wheeler, Candace Thurber, 102
Whiting, Sarah Frances, 102
Who's Who in America, 52, 94, 132
Who's Who of American Women,
    131
Willard, Emma, 84, 103
Willard, Frances E., 78
Wizard of Oz, The, 28
Woman in Sexist Society, 72
Women: in architecture, 15; and
    educational attainment, 15; in
    engineering, 15, 29–30; in
    executive positions, 31, 89, 95,
    111; in labor force, 2, 12–14, 16;
    in professions, 15–19, 87; in
    veterinary medicine, 15; and
    work-life expectancy, 14

Women of Courage, 73
Women-faculty/women-student
    ratio, 131
Women's Christian Temperance
    Union (WTCU), 76, 78
Women's colleges and career
    achievement, 131–32
Women's studies, 71
Woolf, Virginia, 7, 72, 73
Working mothers and mental
    health, 14. *See also* Maternal
    employment; Women, in labor
    force
Wuthering Heights, 7

Yale University, 129–30
Yearling, The, 77

Zajonc, Robert, 97–98